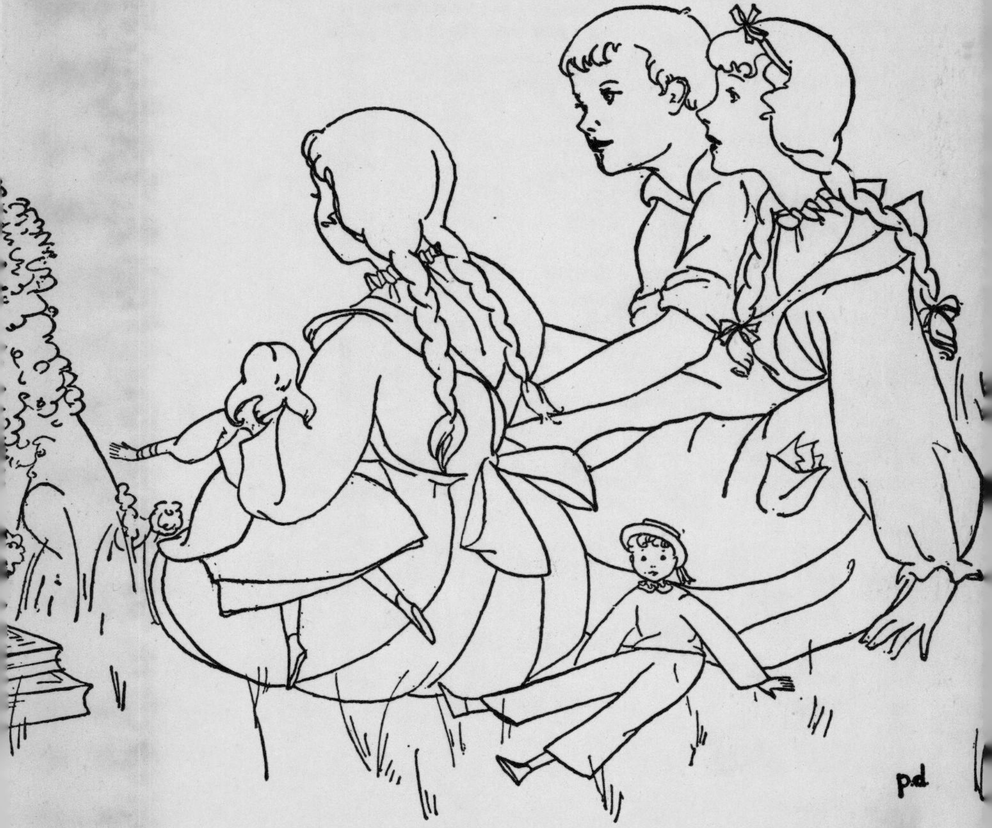
p.d.

Ms. Margaret A. Bartow
3439 Hanville Corners Road
Monroeville, OH 44847-9757

To Ruth Mary
from Grandma
&
Aunt Leona
8/18/40

LULU'S LIBRARY

Sophie clasped the bracelets on her round arms, the necklace about her white throat.

LULU'S LIBRARY

BY
LOUISA M. ALCOTT
Author of "Little Women," etc.

Complete Authorized Edition
Published by arrangement with Little, Brown and Company

GROSSET & DUNLAP
Publishers   New York

Copyright, 1885, 1887,
BY LOUISA M. ALCOTT

Copyright, 1889, 1912, 1914, 1916,
BY JOHN S. P. ALCOTT

Copyright, 1930,
BY LITTLE, BROWN, AND COMPANY

All rights reserved

PRINTED IN THE UNITED STATES OF AMERICA

FOREWORD

WE have all read and enjoyed Miss Alcott's "Little Women" and her other long stories, but few of us are familiar with her first work. The flower fairy tales, written when she was but sixteen years old, were first told to her younger sisters and their neighbors, the little Emersons and Channings, with whom they became such great favorites that she set them down on paper and published them under the title of "Flower Fables." They won for her an unexpected recognition as a writer for children and opened the door of opportunity. Years later, when success was assured and the children were clamoring for more stories, she republished these tales together with those she had told to her little niece during their "quiet hour before bedtime" in a three-volume edition called "Lulu's Library."

The stories in the present collection were selected mainly from the group of fairy tales because they contain delicate flights of fancy and promising bits of colorful description. They are really the ladder upon which Miss Alcott climbed to fame and should be of interest to the girls and boys of to-day as the first effort of an author whose popularity has remained undiminished through the years.

E. G. L.

February, 1930
Los Angeles, California

PREFACE

RECOLLECTIONS OF MY CHILDHOOD

ONE of my earliest memories is of playing with books in my father's study, — building towers and bridges of the big dictionaries, looking at pictures, pretending to read, and scribbling on blank pages whenever pen or pencil could be found. Many of these first attempts at authorship still exist; and I often wonder if these childish plays did not influence my after-life, since books have been my greatest comfort, castle-building a never-failing delight, and scribbling a very profitable amusement.

Another very vivid recollection is of the day when running after my hoop I fell into the Frog Pond and was rescued by a black boy, becoming a friend to the colored race then and there, though my mother always declared that I was an abolitionist at the age of three.

During the Garrison riot in Boston the portrait of George Thompson was hidden under a bed in our house for safe keeping; and I am told that I used to go and comfort " the good man who helped poor slaves" in his captivity. However that may be, the conversion was genuine; and my greatest pride is in the fact that I have lived to know the brave men and women who did so much for the cause, and that I had a very small share in the war which put an end to a great wrong.

Being born on the birthday of Columbus, I seem to have something of my patron saint's spirit of adventure, and running away was one of the delights of my childhood. Many a social lunch have I shared with hospitable Irish beggar children, as we ate our crusts, cold potatoes, and salt fish on voyages of discovery among the ash heaps of the waste land that then lay where the Albany station now stands.

Many an impromptu picnic have I had on the dear old Common, with strange boys, pretty babies, and friendly dogs, who always seemed to feel that this reckless young person needed looking after.

On one occasion the town-crier found me fast asleep at nine o'clock at night, on a doorstep in Bedford Street, with my head pillowed on the curly breast of a big Newfoundland, who was with difficulty persuaded to release the weary little wanderer who had sobbed herself to sleep there.

Preface

I often smile as I pass that door, and never forget to give a grateful pat to every big dog I meet, for never have I slept more soundly than on that dusty step, nor found a better friend than the noble animal who watched over the lost baby so faithfully.

My father's school was the only one I ever went to; and when this was broken up because he introduced methods now all the fashion, our lessons went on at home, for he was always sure of four little pupils who firmly believed in their teacher, though they have not done him all the credit he deserved.

I never liked arithmetic or grammar, and dodged these branches on all occasions; but reading, composition, history, and geography I enjoyed, as well as the stories read to us with a skill which made the dullest charming and useful.

"Pilgrim's Progress," Krummacher's "Parables," Miss Edgeworth, and the best of the dear old fairy tales made that hour the pleasantest of our day. On Sundays we had a simple service of Bible stories, hymns, and conversation about the state of our little consciences and the conduct of our childish lives which never will be forgotten.

Walks each morning round the Common while in the city, and long tramps over hill and dale when our home was in the country, were a part of our education, as well as every sort of housework, for which I have always been very grateful, since such knowledge makes one independent in these days of domestic tribulation with the help who are too often only hindrances.

Needle-work began early; and at ten my skilful sister made a linen shirt beautifully, while at twelve I set up as a dolls' dressmaker, with my sign out, and wonderful models in my window. All the children employed me; and my turbans were the rage at one time, to the great dismay of the neighbor's hens, who were hotly hunted down that I might tweak out their downiest feathers to adorn the dolls' head-gear.

Active exercise was my delight from the time when a child of six I drove my hoop round the Common without stopping, to the days when I did my twenty miles in five hours and went to a party in the evening.

I always thought I must have been a deer or a horse in some former state, because it was such a joy to run. No boy could be my friend till I had beaten him in a race, and no girl if she refused to climb trees, leap fences, and be a tomboy.

My wise mother, anxious to give me a strong body to support a lively brain, turned me loose in the country and let me run wild, learning of Nature what no books can teach, and being led, as those who truly love her seldom fail to be,

> "Through Nature up to Nature's God."

I remember running over the hills just at dawn one summer morning, and pausing to rest in the silent woods, saw, through an arch of trees, the sun rise over river, hill, and wide green meadows as I never saw it before.

Something born of the lovely hour, a happy mood, and the unfolding aspirations of a child's soul seemed to bring me very near to God; and in the hush of that morning hour I always felt that I "got religion," as the phrase goes. A new and vital sense of His presence, tender and sustaining as a father's arms, came to me then, never to change through forty years of life's vicissitudes, but to grow stronger for the sharp discipline of poverty and pain, sorrow and success.

Those Concord days were the happiest of my life, for we had charming playmates in the little Emersons, Channings, Hawthornes, and Goodwins, with the illustrious parents and their friends to enjoy our pranks and share our excursions.

Plays in the barn were a favorite amusement, and

we dramatized the fairy tales in great style. Our giant came tumbling off a loft when Jack cut down the squash-vine running up a ladder to represent the immortal bean. Cinderella rolled away in a vast pumpkin; and a long black pudding was lowered by invisible hands to fasten itself on the nose of the woman who wasted her three wishes.

Little pilgrims journeyed over the hills with script and staff, and cockle-shells in their hats; elves held their pretty revels among the pines, and "Peter Wilkins' " flying ladies came swinging down on the birch tree-tops. Lords and ladies haunted the garden, and mermaids splashed in the bath-house of woven willows over the brook.

People wondered at our frolics, but enjoyed them; and droll stories are still told of the adventures of those days. Mr. Emerson and Margaret Fuller were visiting my parents one afternoon; and the conversation having turned to the ever-interesting subject of education, Miss Fuller said, —

"Well, Mr. Alcott, you have been able to carry out your methods in your own family, and I should like to see your model children."

She did in a few moments, — for as the guests stood on the doorsteps, a wild uproar approached, and round the corner of the house came a wheelbarrow holding baby May arrayed as a queen; I was the horse, bitted and bridled, and driven by my elder sister Anna, while Lizzie played dog and barked as loud as her gentle voice permitted.

All were shouting, and wild with fun, which, however, came to a sudden end as we espied the stately group before us, for my foot tripped, and down we all went in a laughing heap, while my mother put a climax to the joke by saying with a dramatic wave of the hand, —

"Here are the model children, Miss Fuller!"

My sentimental period began at fifteen, when I fell to writing romances, poems, a "heart journal," and dreaming dreams of a splendid future.

Browsing over Mr. Emerson's library, I found "Goethe's Correspondence with a Child," and was at once fired with the desire to be a second Bettine, making my father's friend my Goethe. So I wrote letters to him, but was wise enough never to send them, left wild flowers on the doorsteps of my "Master," sung Mignon's song in very bad German under his window, and was fond of wandering by moonlight, or sitting in a cherry-tree at midnight till the owls scared me to bed.

The girlish folly did not last long, and the letters were burned years ago; but Goethe is still my favorite author, and Emerson remained my beloved "Master" while he lived, doing more for me, as for many another young soul, than he ever knew, by the simple beauty of his life, the truth and wisdom of his books, the example of a good great man untempted and unspoiled by the world which he made nobler while in it, and left the richer when he went.

The trials of life began about this time, and my happy childhood ended. Money is never plentiful in a philosopher's house; and even the maternal pelican could not supply all our wants on the small income which was freely shared with every needy soul who asked for help.

Fugitive slaves were sheltered under our roof; and my first pupil was a very black George Washington whom I taught to write on the hearth with charcoal, his big fingers finding pen and pencil unmanageable.

Motherless girls seeking protection were guarded among us; hungry travellers sent on to our door to be fed and warmed; and if the philosopher happened to own two coats, the best went to a needy brother, for these were practical Christians who had the most perfect faith in Providence, and never found it betrayed.

Preface

In those days the prophets were not honored in their own land, and Concord had not yet discovered her great men. It was a sort of refuge for reformers of all sorts, whom the good natives regarded as lunatics, harmless but amusing.

My father went away to hold his classes and conversations, and we women folk began to feel that we also might do something. So one gloomy November day we decided to move to Boston and try our fate again after some years in the wilderness.

My father's prospect was as promising as a philosopher's ever is in a money-making world; my mother's friends offered her a good salary as their missionary to the poor; and my sister and I hoped to teach. It was an anxious council; and always preferring action to discussion, I took a brisk run over the hill and then settled down for "a good think" in my favorite retreat.

It was an old cart-wheel, half hidden in grass under the locusts where I used to sit to wrestle with my sums, and usually forget them scribbling verses or fairy tales on my slate instead. Perched on the hub, I surveyed the prospect and found it rather gloomy, with leafless trees, sere grass, leaden sky, and frosty air; but the hopeful heart of fifteen beat warmly under the old red shawl, visions of success gave the gray clouds a silver lining, and I said defiantly, as I shook my fist at fate embodied in a crow cawing dismally on a fence near by, —

"I *will* do something by-and-by. Don't care what, teach, sew, act, write, anything to help the family; and I'll be rich and famous and happy before I die, see if I won't!"

Startled by this audacious outburst, the crow flew away; but the old wheel creaked as if it began to turn at that moment, stirred by the intense desire of an ambitious girl to work for those she loved and find some reward when the duty was done.

I did not mind the omen then, and returned to the house cold but resolute. I think I began to shoulder my burden then and there, for when the free country life ended, the wild colt soon learned to tug in harness, only breaking loose now and then for a taste of beloved liberty.

My sisters and I had cherished fine dreams of a home in the city; but when we found ourselves in a small house at the South End with not a tree in sight, only a back yard to play in, and no money to buy any of the splendors before us, we all rebelled and longed for the country again.

Anna soon found little pupils, and trudged away each morning to her daily task, pausing at the corner to wave her hand to me in answer to my salute with the duster. My father went to his classes at his room down town, mother to her all-absorbing poor, the little girls to school, and I was left to keep house, feeling like a caged sea-gull as I washed dishes and cooked in the basement kitchen, where my prospect was limited to a procession of muddy boots.

Good drill, but very hard; and my only consolation was the evening reunion when all met with such varied reports of the day's adventures, we could not fail to find both amusement and instruction.

Father brought news from the upper world, and the wise, good people who adorned it; mother, usually much dilapidated because she *would* give away her clothes, with sad tales of suffering and sin from the darker side of life; gentle Anna a modest account of her success as teacher, for even at seventeen her sweet nature won all who knew her, and her patience quelled the most rebellious pupil.

My reports were usually a mixture of the tragic and the comic; and the children poured their small joys and woes into the family bosom, where comfort and sympathy were always to be found.

Then we youngsters adjourned to the kitchen

for our fun, which usually consisted of writing, dressing, and acting a series of remarkable plays. In one I remember I took five parts and Anna four, with lightning changes of costume, and characters varying from a Greek prince in silver armor to a murderer in chains.

It was good training for memory and fingers, for we recited pages without a fault, and made every sort of property from a harp to a fairy's spangled wings. Later we acted Shakespeare; and Hamlet was my favorite hero, played with a gloomy glare and a tragic stalk which I have never seen surpassed.

But we were now beginning to play our parts on a real stage, and to know something of the pathetic side of life, with its hard facts, irksome duties, many temptations, and the daily sacrifice of self. Fortunately we had the truest, tenderest of guides and guards, and so learned the sweet uses of adversity, the value of honest work, the beautiful law of compensation which gives more than it takes, and the real significance of life.

At sixteen I began to teach twenty pupils, and for ten years learned to know and love children. The story-writing went on all the while with the usual trials of beginners. Fairy tales told the Emersons made the first printed book, and "Hospital Sketches" the first successful one.

Every experience went into the caldron to come out as froth, or evaporate in smoke, till time and suffering strengthened and clarified the mixture of truth and fancy, and a wholesome draught for children began to flow pleasantly and profitably.

So the omen proved a true one, and the wheel of fortune turned slowly, till the girl of fifteen found herself a woman of fifty, with her prophetic dream beautifully realized, her duty done, her reward far greater than she deserved.

LOUISA M. ALCOTT

CONTENTS

THE SILVER PARTY	3
THE SKIPPING SHOES	21
EVA'S VISIT TO FAIRYLAND	34
THE FROST KING AND HOW THE FAIRIES CONQUERED HIM	54
LILYBELL AND THISTLEDOWN, OR THE FAIRY SLEEPING BEAUTY	69
THE CANDY COUNTRY	91
SOPHIE'S SECRET	116
TRUDEL'S SIEGE	151
MUSIC AND MACARONI	186

LULU'S LIBRARY

THE SILVER PARTY

"Such a long morning! Seems as if dinner-time would *never* come!" sighed Tony, as he wandered into the dining-room for a third pick at the nuts and raisins to beguile his weariness with a little mischief.

It was Thanksgiving Day. All the family were at church, all the servants busy preparing for the great dinner; and so poor Tony, who had a cold, had not only to stay at home, but to amuse himself while the rest said their prayers, made calls, or took a brisk walk to get an appetite. If he had been allowed in the kitchen, he would have been quite happy; but cook was busy and cross, and rapped him on the head with a poker when he ventured near the door. Peeping through the slide was also forbidden, and John, the man, bribed him with an orange to keep out of the way till the table was set.

That was now done. The dining-room was empty and quiet, and poor Tony lay down on the sofa to eat his nuts and admire the fine sight before him. All the best damask, china, glass, and silver was set forth with great care. A basket of flowers hung from the chandelier, and the sideboard was beautiful to behold with piled-up fruit, dishes of cake, and many-colored finger-bowls and glasses.

"That's all very nice, but the eating part is what *I* care for. Don't believe I'll get my share to-day, because mamma found out about this horrid cold. A fellow can't help sneezing, though he *can* hide a sore throat. Oh, hum! nearly two more hours to wait;" and with a long sigh Tony closed his eyes for a luxurious yawn.

When he opened them, the strange sight he beheld kept him staring without a thought of sleep. The big soup-ladle stood straight up at the head of the table with a face plainly to be seen in the bright bowl. It was a very heavy, handsome old ladle, so the face was old, but round and jolly; and the long handle stood very erect, like a tall thin gentleman with a big head.

"Well, upon my word that's queer!" said Tony, sitting up also, and wondering what would happen next.

To his great amazement the ladle began to address the assembled forks and spoons in a silvery tone very pleasant to hear: —

"Ladies and gentlemen, at this festive season it is proper that we should enjoy ourselves. As we shall be tired after dinner, we will at once begin our sports by a grand promenade. Take partners and fall in!"

At these words a general uprising took place; and before Tony could get his breath, a long procession of forks and spoons stood ready. The finger-bowls struck up an airy tune as if invisible wet fingers were making music on their rims, and led by the stately ladle like a drum-major, the grand march began. The forks were the gentlemen, tall, slender, and with a fine curve to their backs; the spoons were the ladies, with full skirts, and the scallops on the handles stood up like silver combs; the large ones were the mammas, the teaspoons were the young ladies, and the little salts the children. It was sweet to see the small things walk at the end of the procession, with the two silver rests for the carving knife and fork trotting behind like pet dogs. The mustard-spoon and pickle-fork went together, and quarrelled all the way, both being hot-tempered and sharp-tongued. The steel knives looked on, for this was a very aristocratic party, and only the silver people could join in it.

"Here's fun!" thought Tony, staring with all his might, and so much interested in this remarkable state of things that he forgot hunger and time altogether.

Round and round went the glittering train, to the soft music of the many-toned finger-bowls, till three turns about the long oval table had been made; then all fell into line for a contra-dance, as in the good old times before every one took to spinning like tops. Grandpa Ladle led off with his oldest daughter, Madam Gravy Ladle, and the little salts stood at the bottom prancing like real children impatient for their turn. When it came, they went down the middle in fine style, with a cling! clang! that made Tony's legs quiver with a longing to join in.

It was beautiful to see the older ones twirl round in a stately way, with bows and courtesies at the end, while the teaspoons and small forks romped a good deal, and Mr. Pickle and Miss Mustard kept every one laughing at their smart speeches. The silver butter-knife, who was an invalid, having broken her back and been mended, lay in the rack and smiled sweetly down upon her friends, while the little Cupid on the lid of the butter-dish pirouetted on one toe in the most delightful manner.

When every one had gone through the dance, the napkins were arranged as sofas and the spoons rested, while the polite forks brought sprigs of celery to fan them with. The little salts got into grandpa's lap; and the silver dogs lay down panting, for they had frisked with the children. They all talked; and Tony could not help wondering if real ladies said such things when they put *their* heads together and nodded and whispered, for some of the remarks were so personal that he was much confused. Fortunately they took no notice of him, so he listened and learned something in this queer way.

"I have been in this family a hundred years," began the soup-ladle; "and it seems to me that each generation is worse than the last. My first master was punctual to a minute, and madam was always down beforehand to see that all was ready. Now master comes at all hours; mistress lets the servants do as they like; and the manners of the children are very bad. Sad state of things, very sad!"

"Dear me, yes!" sighed one of the large spoons; "we don't see such nice housekeeping now as we did when we were young. Girls were taught all about it then; but now it is all books or parties, and few of them know a skimmer from a gridiron."

"Well, I'm sure the poor things are much happier than if they were messing about in kitchens as girls used to do in your day. It is much better for them to be dancing, skating, and studying than wasting their young lives darning and preserving, and sitting by their mammas as prim as dishes. *I* prefer the present way of doing things, though the girls in this family *do* sit up too late, and wear too high heels to their boots."

The mustard-spoon spoke in a pert tone, and the pickle-fork answered sharply, —

"I agree with you, cousin. The boys also sit up too late. I'm tired of being waked to fish out olives or pickles for those fellows when they come in from the theatre or some dance; and as for that Tony, he is a real pig, — eats everything he can lay hands on, and is the torment of the maid's life."

"Yes," cried one little salt-spoon, "we saw him steal cake out of the sideboard, and he never told when his mother scolded Norah."

"So mean!" added the other; and both the round faces were so full of disgust that Tony fell flat and shut his eyes as if asleep to hide his confusion. Some one laughed; but he dared not look, and lay blushing and listening to remarks which plainly proved how careful we should be of our acts and words even when alone, for who knows what apparently dumb thing may be watching us.

"I have observed that Mr. Murry reads the paper at table instead of talking to his family; that Mrs.

Murry worries about the servants; the girls gossip and giggle; the boys eat, and plague one another; and that small child Nelly teases for all she sees, and is never quiet till she gets the sugar-bowl," said Grandpa Ladle, in a tone of regret. "Now, useful and pleasant chat at table would make meals delightful, instead of being scenes of confusion and discomfort."

"I bite their tongues when I get a chance, hoping to make them witty or to check unkind words; but they only sputter, and get a lecture from Aunt Maria, who is a sour old spinster, always criticising her neighbors."

As the mustard-spoon spoke, the teaspoons laughed as if they thought *her* rather like Aunt Maria in that respect.

"I gave the baby a fit of colic to teach her to let pickles alone, but no one thanked me," said the pickle-fork.

"Perhaps if we keep ourselves so bright that those who use us can see their faces in us, we shall be able to help them a little; for no one likes to see an ugly face or a dull spoon. The art of changing frowns to smiles is never old-fashioned; and lovely manners smooth away the little worries of life beautifully." A silvery voice spoke, and all looked respectfully at Madam Gravy Ladle, who was a very fine old spoon, with a coat of arms on it, and a polish that all envied.

"People can't always be remembering how old and valuable and bright they are. Here in America we just go ahead and make manners and money for ourselves. *I* don't stop to ask what dish I'm going to help to empty; I just pitch in and take all I can hold, and don't care a bit whether I shine or not. My grandfather was a kitchen spoon; but I'm smarter than he was, thanks to my plating, and look and feel as good as any one, though I haven't got stags' heads and big letters on my handle."

No one answered these impertinent remarks of the sauce-spoon, for all knew that she was not pure silver, and was only used on occasions when many spoons were needed. Tony was ashamed to hear her talk in that rude way to the fine old silver he was so proud of, and resolved he'd give the saucy spoon a good rap when he helped himself to the cranberry.

An impressive silence lasted till a lively fork exclaimed, as the clock struck, "Every one is coasting out-of-doors. Why not have our share of the fun inside? It is very fashionable this winter, and ladies and gentlemen of the best families do it, I assure you."

"We will!" cried the other forks; and as the dowagers did not object, all fell to work to arrange the table for this agreeable sport. Tony sat up to see how they would manage, and was astonished at the ingenuity of the silver people. With a great clinking and rattling they ran to and fro, dragging the stiff white mats about; the largest they leaned up against the tall caster, and laid the rest in a long slope to the edge of the table, where a pile of napkins made a nice snowdrift to tumble into.

"What *will* they do for sleds?" thought Tony; and the next minute chuckled when he saw them take the slices of bread laid at each place, pile on, and spin away, with a great scattering of crumbs like snowflakes, and much laughter as they landed in the white pile at the end of the coast.

"Won't John give it to 'em if he comes in and catches 'em turning his nice table topsy-turvy!" said the boy to himself, hoping nothing would happen to end this jolly frolic. So he kept very still, and watched the gay forks and spoons climb up and whiz down till they were tired. The little salts got Baby Nell's own small slice, and had lovely times on a short coast of their own made of one mat held up by grandpa, who smiled benevolently at the fun, being too old and heavy to join in it.

They kept it up until the slices were worn thin, and one or two upsets alarmed the ladies; then they rested and conversed again. The mammas talked about their children, how sadly the silver basket needed a new lining, and what there was to be for dinner. The teaspoons whispered sweetly together, as young ladies do, — one declaring that rouge powder was not as good as it used to be, another lamenting the sad effect of eggs upon her complexion, and all smiled amiably upon the forks, who stood about discussing wines and cigars, for both lived in the sideboard, and were brought out after dinner, so the forks knew a great deal about such matters, and found them very interesting, as all gentlemen seem to do.

Presently some one mentioned bicycles, and what fine rides the boys of the family told about. The other fellows proposed a race; and before Tony could grasp the possibility of such a thing, it was done. Nothing easier, for there stood a pile of plates, and just turning them on their edges, the forks got astride, and the big wheels spun away as if a whole bicycle club had suddenly arrived.

Old Pickle took the baby's plate, as better suited to his size. The little salts made a tricycle of napkin-rings, and rode gayly off, with the dogs barking after them. Even the carving-fork, though not invited, could not resist the exciting sport, and tipping up the wooden bread-platter, went whizzing off at a great pace, for his two prongs were better than four, and his wheel was lighter than the china ones. Grandpapa Ladle cheered them on, like a fine old gentleman as he was, for though the new craze rather astonished him, he liked manly sports, and would have taken a turn if his dignity and age had allowed. The ladies chimed their applause, for it really was immensely exciting to see fourteen plates with forks astride racing round the large table with cries of, "Go it, Pickle! Now, then, Prongs! Steady, Silver-top! Hurrah for the twins!"

The fun was at its height when young Prongs ran against Pickle, who did not steer well, and both went off the table with a crash. All stopped at once, and crowded to the edge to see who was killed. The plates lay in pieces, old Pickle had a bend in his back that made him groan dismally, and Prongs had fallen down the register.

Wails of despair arose at that awful sight, for he was a favorite with every one, and such a tragic death was too much for some of the tender-hearted spoons, who fainted at the idea of that gallant fork's destruction in what to them was a fiery volcano.

"Serves Pickle right! He ought to know he was too old for such wild games," scolded Miss Mustard, peering anxiously over at her friend, for they were fond of one another in spite of their tiffs.

"Now let us see what these fine folks will do when they get off the damask and come to grief. A helpless lot, I fancy, and those fellows deserve what they've got," said the sauce-spoon, nearly upsetting the twins as she elbowed her way to the front to jeer over the fallen.

"I think you will see that gentle people are as brave as those who make a noise," answered Madam Gravy, and leaning over the edge of the table she added in her sweet voice, "Dear Mr. Pickle, we will let down a napkin and pull you up if you have strength to take hold."

"Pull away, ma'am," groaned Pickle, who well deserved his name just then, and soon, thanks to Madam's presence of mind, he was safely laid on a pile of mats, while Miss Mustard put a plaster on his injured back.

Meanwhile brave Grandpapa Ladle had slipped from the table to a chair, and so to the floor with-

The Silver Party

out too great a jar to his aged frame; then sliding along the carpet, he reached the register. Peering down that dark, hot abyss he cried, while all listened breathlessly for a reply, "Prongs, my boy, are you there?"

"Ay, ay, sir; I'm caught in the wire screen. Ask some of the fellows to lend a hand and get me out before I'm melted," answered the fork, with a gasp of agony.

Instantly the long handle of the patriarchal Ladle was put down to his rescue, and after a moment of suspense, while Prongs caught firmly hold, up he came, hot and dusty, but otherwise unharmed by that dreadful fall. Cheers greeted them, and every one lent a hand at the napkin as they were hoisted to the table to be embraced by their joyful relatives and friends.

"What did you think about down in that horrid place?" asked one of the twins.

"I thought of a story I once heard master tell, about a child who was found one cold day sitting with his feet on a newspaper, and when asked what he was doing, answered, 'Warming my feet on the "Christian Register."' I hoped my register would be Christian enough not to melt me before help came. Ha! ha! See the joke, my dears?" and Prongs laughed as gayly as if he never had taken a header into a volcano.

"What did you see down there?" asked the other twin, curious, as all small people are.

"Lots of dust and pins, a doll's head baby put there, Norah's thimble, and the big red marble that boy Tony was raging about the other day. It's a regular catch-all, and shows how the work is shirked in this house," answered Prongs, stretching his legs, which were a little damaged by the fall.

"What shall we do about the plates?" asked Pickle, from his bed.

"Let them lie, for we can't mend them. John will think the boy broke them, and he'll get punished, as he deserves, for he broke a tumbler yesterday, and put it slyly in the ash-barrel," said Miss Mustard, spitefully.

"Oh! I say, that's mean," began Tony; but no one listened, and in a minute Prongs answered bravely, —

"I'm a gentleman, and I don't let other people take the blame of my scrapes. Tony has enough of his own to answer for."

"I'll have that bent fork for mine, and make John keep it as bright as a new dollar to pay for this. Prongs is a trump, and I wish I could tell him so," thought Tony, much gratified at this handsome behavior.

"Right, grandson. I am pleased with you; but allow me to suggest that the Chinese Mandarin on the chimney-piece be politely requested to mend the plates. He can do that sort of thing nicely, and will be charmed to oblige us, I am sure."

Grandpapa's suggestion was a good one; and Yam Ki Lo consented at once, skipped to the floor, tapped the bits of china with his fan, and in the twinkling of an eye was back on his perch, leaving two whole plates behind him, for he was a wizard, and knew all about blue china.

Just as the silver people were rejoicing over this fine escape from discovery, the clock struck, a bell rang, voices were heard upstairs, and it was very evident that the family had arrived.

At these sounds a great flurry arose in the dining-room, as every spoon, fork, plate, and napkin flew back to its place. Pickle rushed to the jar, and plunged in head first, regardless of his back; Miss Mustard retired to the caster; the twins scrambled into the salt-cellar; and the silver dogs lay down by the carving knife and fork as quietly as if they had never stirred a leg; Grandpapa slowly reposed in his usual place; Madam followed his example with dignity; the teaspoons climbed into the holder, uttering little cries of alarm; and Prongs stayed to help them till he had barely time to drop down at Tony's place, and lie there with his bent leg in the air, the only sign of the great fall, about which he talked for a long time afterward. All was in order but the sauce-spoon, who had stopped to laugh at the Mandarin till it was too late to get to her corner; and before she could find any place of concealment, John came in and caught her lying in the middle of the table, looking very common and shabby among all the bright silver.

"What in the world is that old plated thing here for? Missis told Norah to put it in the kitchen, as she had a new one for a present to-day — real silver — so out you go;" and as he spoke, John threw the spoon through the slide, — an exile forevermore from the good society which she did not value as she should.

Tony saw the glimmer of a smile in Grandpapa Ladle's face, but it was gone like a flash, and by the time the boy reached the table nothing was to be seen in the silver bowl but his own round rosy countenance, full of wonder.

"I don't think any one will believe what I've

seen, but I mean to tell, it was so *very* curious," he said, as he surveyed the scene of the late frolic, now so neat and quiet that not a wrinkle or a crumb betrayed what larks had been going on.

Hastily fishing up his long-lost marble, the doll's head, and Norah's thimble, he went thoughtfully upstairs to welcome his cousins, still much absorbed by this very singular affair.

Dinner was soon announced; and while it lasted, every one was too busy eating the good things befor them to observe how quiet the usually riotous Tony was. His appetite for turkey and cranberries seemed to have lost its sharp edge, and the mince-pie must have felt itself sadly slighted by his lack of appreciation of its substance and flavor. He seemed in a brown-study, and kept staring about as if he saw more than other people did. He examined Nelly's plate as if looking for a crack, smiled at the little spoon when he took salt, refused pickles and mustard with a frown, kept a certain bent fork by him as long as possible, and tried to make music with a wet finger on the rim of his bowl at dessert.

But in the evening, when the young people sat around the fire, he amused them by telling the queer story of the silver party; but he very wisely left out the remarks made upon himself and family, remembering how disagreeable the sauce-spoon had seemed, and he privately resolved to follow Madam Gravy Ladle's advice to keep his own face bright, manners polite, and speech kindly, that he might prove himself to be pure silver, and be stamped a gentleman.

THE SKIPPING SHOES

ONCE there was a little girl, named Kitty, who never wanted to do what people asked her. She said "I won't" and "I can't," and did not run at once pleasantly, as obliging children do.

One day her mother gave her a pair of new shoes; and after a fuss about putting them on, Kitty said, as she lay kicking on the floor, —

"I wish these were seven-leagued boots, like Jack the Giant Killer's; then it would be easy to run errands all the time. Now, I hate to keep trotting, and I don't like new shoes, and I won't stir a step."

Just as she said that, the shoes gave a skip, and set her on her feet so suddenly that it scared all the naughtiness out of her. She stood looking at these curious shoes; and the bright buttons on them seemed to wink at her like eyes, while the heels tapped on the floor a sort of tune. Before she dared to stir, her mother called from the next room, —

"Kitty, run and tell the cook to make a pie for dinner; I forgot it."

"I don't want to," began Kitty, with a whine as usual.

But the words were hardly out of her mouth when the shoes gave one jump, and took her downstairs, through the hall, and landed her at the kitchen door. Her breath was nearly gone; but she gave the message, and turned round, trying to see if the shoes would let her walk at all. They went nicely till she wanted to turn into the china-closet where the cake was. She was forbidden to touch it, but loved to take a bit when she could. Now she found that her feet were fixed fast to the floor, and could not be moved till her father said, as he passed the window close by, —

"You will have time to go to the post-office before school and get my letters."

"I can't," began Kitty; but she found she could, for away went the shoes, out of the house at one bound, and trotted down the street so fast that the maid who ran after her with her hat could not catch her.

"I can't stop!" cried Kitty; and she did not till the shoes took her straight into the office.

"What's the hurry to-day?" asked the man, as he saw her without any hat, all rosy and breathless, and her face puckered up as if she did not know whether to laugh or to cry.

"I won't tell any one about these dreadful shoes, and I'll take them off as soon as I get home. I hope

The Skipping Shoes

they will go back slowly, or people will think I'm crazy," said Kitty to herself, as she took the letters and went away.

The shoes walked nicely along till she came to the bridge; and there she wanted to stop and watch some boys in a boat, forgetting school and her father's letters. But the shoes wouldn't stop, though she tried to make them, and held on to the railing as hard as she could. Her feet went on; and when she sat down, they still dragged her along so steadily that she had to go, and she got up feeling that there was something very strange about these shoes. The minute she gave up, all went smoothly, and she got home in good time.

"I won't wear these horrid things another minute," said Kitty, sitting on the doorstep and trying to unbutton the shoes.

But not a button could she stir, though she got red and angry struggling to do it.

"Time for school; run away, little girl," called mamma from upstairs, as the clock struck nine.

"I won't!" said Kitty, crossly.

But she did; for those magic shoes danced her off, and landed her at her desk in five minutes.

"Well, I'm not late; that's one comfort," she thought, wishing she had come pleasantly, and not been whisked away without any luncheon.

Her legs were so tired with the long skips that she was glad to sit still; and that pleased the teacher, for generally she was fussing about all lesson time. But at recess she got into trouble again; for one of the children knocked down the house of corn-cobs she had built, and made her angry.

"Now, I'll kick yours down, and see how you like it, Dolly."

Up went her foot, but it didn't come down; it stayed in the air, and there she stood looking as if she were going to dance. The children laughed to see her, and she could do nothing till she said to Dolly in a great hurry, —

"Never mind; if you didn't mean to, I'll forgive you."

Then the foot went down, and Kitty felt so glad about it that she tried to be pleasant, fearing some new caper of those dreadful shoes. She began to see how they worked, and thought she would try if she had any power over them. So, when one of the children wanted his ball, which had bounced over the hedge, she said kindly, —

"Perhaps I can get it for you, Willy."

And over she jumped as lightly as if she too were an india-rubber ball.

"How could you do it?" cried the boys, much

The Skipping Shoes 25

surprised; for not one of them dared try such a high leap.

Kitty laughed, and began to dance, feeling pleased and proud to find there was a good side to the shoes after all. Such twirlings and skippings as she made, such pretty steps and airy little bounds it was pretty to see; for it seemed as if her feet were bewitched, and went of themselves. The little girls were charmed, and tried to imitate her; but no one could, and they stood in a circle watching her dance till the bell rang; then all rushed in to tell about it.

Kitty said it was her new shoes, and never told how queerly they acted, hoping to have good times now. But she was mistaken.

On the way home she wanted to stop and see her friend Bell's new doll; but at the gate her feet stuck fast, and she had to give up her wishes and go straight on, as mamma had told her always to do.

"Run and pick a nice little dish of strawberries for dinner," said her sister, as she went in.

"I'm too ti — " There was no time to finish, for the shoes landed her in the middle of the strawberry bed at one jump.

"I might as well be a grasshopper if I'm to skip round like this," she said, forgetting to feel tired out there in the pleasant garden, with the robins picking berries close by, and a cool wind lifting the leaves to show where the reddest and ripest ones hid.

The little dish was soon filled, and she wanted to stay and eat a few, warm and sweet from the vines; but the bell rang, and away she went, over the wood-pile, across the piazza, and into the dining-room before the berry in her mouth was half eaten.

"How this child does rush about to-day!" said her mother. "It is so delightful to have such a quick little errand-girl that I shall get her to carry some bundles to my poor people this afternoon."

"Oh, dear me! I do hate to lug those old clothes and bottles and baskets of cold victuals round. Must I do it?" sighed Kitty, dismally, while the shoes tapped on the floor under the table, as if to remind her that she must, whether she liked it or not.

"It would be right and kind, and would please me very much. But you may do as you choose about it. I am very tired, and some one must go; for the little Bryan baby is sick and needs what I send," said mamma, looking disappointed.

Kitty sat very still and sober for some time, and no one spoke to her. She was making up her mind whether she would go pleasantly or be whisked about like a grasshopper against her will. When dinner was over, she said in a cheerful voice, —

"I'll go, mamma; and when all the errands are done, may I come back through Fairyland, as we call the little grove where the tall ferns grow?"

"Yes, dear; when you oblige me, I am happy to please you."

"I'm glad I decided to be good; now I shall have a lovely time," said Kitty to herself, as she trotted away with a basket in one hand, a bundle in the other, and some money in her pocket for a poor old woman who needed help.

The shoes went quietly along, and seemed to know just where to stop. The sick baby's mother thanked her for the soft little nightgowns; the lame girl smiled when she saw the books; the hungry children gathered round the basket of food, like young birds eager to be fed; and the old woman gave her a beautiful pink shell that her sailor son brought home from sea.

When all the errands were done, Kitty skipped away to Fairyland, feeling very happy, as people always do when they have done kind things. It was a lovely place; for the ferns made green arches tall enough for little girls to sit under, and the ground was covered with pretty green moss and wood-flowers. Birds flew about in the pines, squirrels chattered in the oaks, butterflies floated here and there, and from the pond near by came the croak of frogs sunning their green backs on the mossy stones.

"I wonder if the shoes will let me stop and rest; it is so cool here, and I'm so tired," said Kitty, as she came to a cozy nook at the foot of a tree.

The words were hardly out of her mouth when her feet folded under her, and there she sat on a cushion of moss, like the queen of the wood on her throne. Something lighted with a bump close by her; and looking down she saw a large black cricket with a stiff tail, staring at her curiously.

"Bless my heart! I thought you were some relation of my cousin Grasshopper's. You came down the hill with long leaps just like him; so I stopped to say, How d' ye do," said the cricket in its creaky voice.

"I'm not a grasshopper; but I have on fairy shoes to-day, and so do many things that I never did before," answered Kitty, much surprised to be able to understand what the cricket said.

"It is midsummer day, and fairies can play whatever pranks they like. If you didn't have those shoes on, you couldn't understand what I say. Hark, and hear those squirrels talk, and the birds, and the ants down here. Make the most of this chance; for at sunset your shoes will stop skipping, and the fun all be over."

While the cricket talked, Kitty did hear all sorts of little voices, singing, laughing, chatting in the gayest way, and understood every word they said. The squirrels called to one another as they raced about, —

"Here's a nut, there's a nut;
  Hide it quick away,
In a hole, under leaves,
  To eat some winter day.
Acorns sweet are plenty,
  We will have them all:
Skip and scamper lively
  Till the last ones fall."

The birds were singing softly, —

"Rock a bye, babies,
  Your cradle hangs high;
Soft down your pillow,
  Your curtain the sky.
Father will feed you,
  While mother will sing,
And shelter our darlings
  With her warm wing."

And the ants were saying to one another as they hurried in and out of their little houses, —

"Work, neighbor, work!
　Do not stop to play;
Wander far and wide,
　Gather all you may.
We are never like
　Idle butterflies,
But like the busy bees,
　Industrious and wise."

"Ants always were dreadfully good, but butterflies are ever so much prettier," said Kitty, listening to the little voices with wonder and pleasure.

"Hollo! hollo!
Come down below, —
It's lovely and cool
Out here in the pool;
On a lily-pad float
For a nice green boat.
Here we sit and sing
In a pleasant ring;
Or leap-frog play,
In the jolliest way.
Our games have begun,
Come join in the fun."

"Dear me! what could I do over there in the mud with the queer green frogs?" laughed Kitty, as this song was croaked at her.

> "No, no, come and fly
> Through the sunny sky,
> Or honey sip
> From the rose's lip,
> Or dance in the air,
> Like spirits fair.
> Come away, come away;
> 'T is our holiday."

A cloud of lovely yellow butterflies flew up from a wild-rose bush, and went dancing away higher and higher, till they vanished in the light beyond the wood.

"That is better than leap-frog. I wish my skipping shoes would let me fly up somewhere, instead of carrying me on errands and where I ought to go all the time," said Kitty, watching the pretty things glitter as they flew.

Just at that minute a clock struck, and away went the shoes over the pool, the hill, the road, till they pranced in at the gate as the tea-bell rang. Kitty amused the family by telling what she had done and seen; but no one believed the Fairyland part, and her father said, laughing, —

"Go on, my dear, making up little stories, and by and by you may be as famous as Hans Christian Andersen, whose books you like so well."

"The sun will soon set, and then my fun will be over; so I must skip while I can," thought Kitty, and went waltzing round the lawn so prettily that all the family came to see her.

"She dances so well that she shall go to dancing-school," said her mother, pleased with the pretty antics of her little girl.

Kitty was delighted to hear that; for she had longed to go, and went on skipping as hard as she could, that she might learn some of the graceful steps the shoes took before the day was done.

"Come, dear, stop now, and run up to your bath and bed. It has been a long hot day, and you are tired; so get to sleep early, for Nursey wants to go out," said her mother, as the sun went down behind the hills with a last bright glimmer, like the wink of a great sleepy eye.

"Oh, please, a few minutes more," began Kitty, but was off like a flash; for the shoes trotted her upstairs so fast that she ran against old Nursey, and down she went, splashing the water all over the floor, and scolding in such a funny way that it made Kitty laugh so that she could hardly pick her up again.

By the time she was ready to undress the sun was quite gone, and the shoes she took off were common ones again, for midsummer day was over. But Kitty never forgot the little lessons she had learned: she tried to run willingly when spoken to; she remembered the pretty steps and danced like a fairy; and best of all, she always loved the innocent and interesting little creatures in the woods and fields, and whenever she was told she might go to play with them, she hurried away almost as quickly as if she still wore the skipping shoes.

EVA'S VISIT TO FAIRYLAND

A LITTLE girl lay on the grass down by the brook wondering what the brown water said as it went babbling over the stones. As she listened, she heard another kind of music that seemed to come nearer and nearer, till round the corner floated a beautiful boat filled with elves, who danced on the broad green leaves of the lily of the valley, while the white bells of the tall stem that was the mast rung loud and sweet.

A flat rock, covered with moss, stood in the middle of the brook, and here the boat was anchored for the elves to rest a little. Eva watched them at their pretty play, as they flew about or lay fanning themselves and drinking from the red-brimmed cups on the rocks. Wild strawberries grew in the grass close by, and Eva threw some of the ripest to the fairy folk; for honey and dew seemed a poor sort of lunch to the child. Then the elves saw her, and nodded and smiled and called, but their soft voices could not reach her. So, after whispering among themselves, two of them flew to the brookside, and perching on a buttercup said close to Eva's ear, —

"We have come to thank you for your berries, and to ask if we can do anything for you, because this is our holiday and we can become visible to you."

"Oh, let me go to Fairyland! I have longed so to see and know all about your dear little people; and never would believe it is true that there are no fairies left," cried Eva, so glad to find that she was right.

"We should not dare to take some children, they would do so much harm; but you believe in us, you love all the sweet things in the world, and never hurt innocent creatures, or tread on flowers, or let ugly passions come into your happy little heart. You shall go with us and see how we live."

But as the elves spoke, Eva looked very sad and said, —

"How can I go? I am so big I should sink that pretty ship with one finger, and I have no wings."

The elves laughed and touched her with their soft hands, saying, —

"You cannot hurt us now. Look in the water and see what we have done."

Eva looked and saw a tiny child standing under a tall blue violet. It was herself, but so small she seemed an elf in a white pinafore and little pink sun-bonnet. She clapped her hands and skipped for joy, and laughed at the cunning picture; but suddenly she grew sober again, as she looked from the shore to the rock.

"But now I am so wee I cannot step over, and you cannot lift me, I am sure."

"Give us each a hand and do not be afraid," said the elves, and whisked her across like dandelion down.

The elves were very glad to see her, and touched and peeped and asked questions as if they had never had a mortal child to play with before. Eva was so small she could dance with them now, and eat what they ate, and sing their pretty songs. She found that flower-honey and dewdrops were very nice, and that it was fine fun to tilt on a blade of grass, to slide down a smooth bulrush-stem, or rock in the cup of a flower. She learned new and merry games, found out what the brook said, saw a cowslip blossom, and had a lovely time till the captain of the ship blew a long sweet blast on a honeysuckle horn, and all the elves went aboard and set sail for home.

"Now I shall find the way to Fairyland and can go again whenever I like," thought Eva, as she floated away.

Eva's Visit to Fairyland

But the sly little people did not mean that she should know, for only now and then can a child go to that lovely place. So they set the bells to chiming softly, and all sung lullabies till Eva fell fast asleep, and knew nothing of the journey till she woke in Fairyland.

It seemed to be sunset; for the sky was red, the flowers all dreaming behind their green curtains, the birds tucked up in their nests, and there was no sound but the whisper of the wind that softly sang, "Good-night, good-night."

"We all go early to bed unless the moon shines. We are tired, so come and let us make you cozy till to-morrow," said the elves, showing her a dainty bed with white rose-leaves for sheets, a red rose-leaf for coverlet, and two plump little mushrooms for pillows. Cobweb curtains hung over it, a glow-worm was the candle, and a lily-of-the-valley cup made a nice nightcap, while a tiny gown of woven thistle-down lay ready to be put on.

Eva quickly undressed and slipped into the pretty bed, where she lay looking at the red light till sleep kissed her eyelids, and a lovely dream floated through her mind till morning came.

As soon as the sun peeped over the hills, the elves were up and away to the lake, where they all dipped and splashed and floated and frolicked till the air was full of sparkling drops and the water white with foam. Then they wiped on soft cobweb towels, which they spread on the grass to dry, while they combed their pretty hair and put on fresh gowns of flower-leaves. After that came breakfast, all sitting about in parties to eat fruit and cakes of pollen, while their drink was fresh dew.

"Now, Eva, you see that we are not idle, foolish creatures, but have many things to do, many lessons to learn, and a heaven of our own to hope for," said the elves when they had all sung together; while the wind, who was the house-maid there, cleared the tables by blowing everything away at one breath. "First of all come to our hospital, — for here we bring all the sick and hurt things cruel or careless people have harmed. In your world children often torment and kill poor birds and worms and flies, and pick flowers to throw away, and chase butterflies till their poor wings are broken. All these we care for, and our magic makes them live again. Come and see."

Eva followed to a cool, quiet place, where on soft beds lay many wounded things. Rose, the fairy nurse, was binding up the leg of a fly as he lay in a cobweb hammock and feebly buzzed his thanks.

In another place an ugly worm was being put together after a cruel boy had cut him in two. Eva thought the elves were good to do such work, and went on to a humming-bird which lay in a bed of honeysuckles, with the quick colors very dim on its little breast and bright wings very still.

"I was shot with an air-gun, and my poor head still aches with the dreadful blow," sighed the poor bird, trying to sip a little honey with his long beak.

"I'm nearly well," chirped a cricket, whose stiff tail had been pulled off by a naughty child and nicely put on again by a very skilful elf.

He looked so cheerful and lively as he hopped about on his bed of dried grass, with his black eyes twinkling, and a bandage of bind-weed holding his tail firmly in place till it was well, that Eva laughed aloud, and at the pleasant sound all the sick things smiled and seemed better.

Rows of pale flowers stood in one place, and elves watered them, or tied up broken leaves, or let in the sunshine to cure their pains, — for these delicate invalids needed much care; and Mignonette was the name of the nurse who watched over them, like a little Sister of Charity, with her gray gown and sweet face.

"You have seen enough. Come to school now, and see where we are taught all that fairies must know," said Trip, the elf who was guiding her about.

In a pleasant place they found the child elves sitting on pink daisies with their books of leaves in their hands, while the teacher was a Jack-in-the-pulpit, who asked questions, and was very wise. Eva nodded to the little ones, and they smiled at the stranger as they rustled their books and pretended to study busily.

A class in arithmetic was going on, and Eva listened to questions that none but elves would care to know.

"Twinkle, if there were fifteen seeds on a dandelion, and the wind blew ten away, how many would be left?"

"Five."

"Bud, if a rose opens three leaves one day, two the next, and seven the next, how many in all?"

"Eleven."

"Daisy, if a silk-worm spins one yard of fairy cloth in an hour, how many can he spin in a day?"

"Twelve, if he isn't lazy," answered the little elf, fluttering her wings, as if anxious to be done.

"Now we will read," said Jack, and a new class

Eva's Visit to Fairyland

flew to the long leaf, where they stood in a row, with open books, ready to begin.

"You may read 'The Flower's Lesson' to-day, and be careful not to sing-song, Poppy," said the teacher, passing a dainty book to Eva that she might follow the story.

"Once there was a rose who had two little buds. One was happy and contented, but the other always wanted something.

" 'I wish the elves would bring me a star instead of dew every night. The drop is soon gone, but a star would shine splendidly, and I should be finer than all the other flowers,' said the naughty bud one night.

" 'But you need the dew to live, and the moon needs the stars up there to light the world. Don't fret, sister, but be sure it is best to take what is sent, and be glad,' answered the good bud.

" 'I won't have the dew, and if I cannot get a star, I will take a firefly to shine on my breast,' said the other, shaking off a fresh drop that had just fallen on her, and folding her leaves round the bright fly.

" 'Foolish child!' cried the rose-mother; 'let the fly go, before he harms you. It is better to be sweet and fair than to shine with a beauty not your own. Be wise, dear, before it is too late.'

"But the silly bud only held the firefly closer, till in its struggles it tore her leaves and flew away. When the hot sun came up, the poor bud hung all faded on her stem, longing for a cool drop to drink. Her sister was strong and fresh, and danced gayly in the wind, opening her red petals to the sun.

" 'Now I must die. Oh, why was I vain and silly?' sobbed the poor bud, fainting in the heat.

"Then the mother leaned over her, and from her bosom, where she had hidden it, the dew-drop fell on the thirsty bud, and while she drank it eagerly, the rose drew her closer, whispering, 'Little darling, learn to be contented with what heaven sends, and make yourself lovely by being good.' "

"I shall remember that story," said Eva when the elves shut their books and flew back to the daisy seats.

"Would you like to hear them sing?" asked Trip.

"Very much," said Eva, and in the little song they gave her she got another lesson to carry home.

"I shine," says the sun,
  "To give the world light,"
"I glimmer," adds the moon,
  "To beautify the night,"

"I ripple," says the brook,
"I whisper," sighs the breeze,
"I patter," laughs the rain,
"We rustle," call the trees.
"We dance," nod the daisies,
"I twinkle," shines the star,
"We sing," chant the birds,
"How happy we all are!"
"I smile," cries the child,
Gentle, good, and gay;
The sweetest thing of all,
The sunshine of each day.

"I shall sing that to myself and try to do my part," said Eva, as the elves got out their paints and brushes of butterfly-down, and using large white leaves for paper, learned to imitate the colors of every flower.

"Why do they do this?" asked Eva, for she saw no pictures anywhere.

"We keep the flowers fresh, for in the world below they have trials with the hot sun that fades, the mould that spots, grubs that gnaw, and frost that bites. We melt bits of rainbow in our paint-pots, and when it is needed, we brighten the soft color on Anemone's cheeks, deepen the blue of Violet's eyes, or polish up the cowslips till they shine like cups of gold. We redden the autumn leaves, and put the purple bloom on the grapes. We make the budding birches a soft green, color maple keys, and hang brown tassels on the alder twigs. We repair the dim spots on butterflies' wings, paint the bluebird like the sky, give Robin his red vest, and turn the yellow bird to a flash of sunshine. Oh, we are artists, and hereafter you will see our pictures everywhere."

"How lovely!" said Eva. "I often wondered who kept all these delicate things so beautiful and gay. But where are we going now?" she added, as the elves led her away from the school.

"Come and see where we learn to ride," they answered, smiling as if they enjoyed this part of their education.

In a little dell where the ground was covered with the softest moss, Eva found the fairy riding-school and gymnasium. The horses were all kinds of winged and swift-footed things, and the race-ground was a smooth path round the highest mound. Groups of elves lay on the ground, swung on the grass-blades, or sat in the wood flowers, that stood all about.

In one place the mothers and fathers were teaching their little ones to fly. The baby elves sat in a row on the branch of a birch-tree, fluttering their small wings and nestling close together, timid yet longing to launch boldly out into the air and float as the others did. The parents were very patient, and one by one the babies took little flights, getting braver and braver each time.

One very timid elf would not stir, so the sly papa and mamma put it on a leaf, and each taking a side, they rode the dear about for a few minutes, till she was used to the motion; then they dropped the leaf, and the little elf finding herself falling spread her wings and flew away to a tall bush, to the great delight of all who saw it.

But the riding was very funny, and Eva soon forgot everything else in watching the gay creatures mount their various horses and fly or gallop round the ring while the teacher — a small fellow in a gay cap and green suit — stood on the moss-mound, cracking a long whip and telling them how to ride in the best fairy fashion.

Several lady elves learned to mount butterflies gracefully and float where they liked, sitting firmly when the winged horses alighted on the flowers. The boy elves preferred field-mice, who went very swiftly round and round, with saddles of woven grass and reins of yellow bind-weed, which looked well on the little gray creatures, who twinkled their bright eyes and whisked their long tails as if they liked it.

But the best fun of all was when the leaping began; and Eva quite trembled lest some sad accident should happen; for grasshoppers were led out, and the gallant elves leaped over the highest flower-tops without falling off.

It was very funny to see the queer hoppers skip with their long legs, and when Puck, the riding-master, mounted, and led a dozen of his pupils a race round the track, all the rest of the elves laughed aloud and clapped their hands in great glee; for Puck was a famous fairy, and his pranks were endless.

Eva was shouting with the rest as the green horses came hopping by, when Puck caught her up before him, and away they raced so swiftly that her hair whistled in the wind and her breath was nearly gone. A tremendous leap took them high over the little hill and landed Eva in a tall dandelion, where she lay laughing and panting as if on a little yellow sofa, while Trip and her mates fanned her and smoothed her pretty hair.

"That was splendid!" she cried. "I wish I was a real fairy, and always lived in this lovely place. Everything will seem so ugly and big and coarse when I go home I shall never be happy again."

"Oh, yes, you will," answered Trip, "for after this visit you will be able to hear and see and know what others never do, and that will make you happy and good. You believed in us, and we reward all who love what we love, and enjoy the beautiful world they live in as we do."

"Thank you," said Eva. "If I can know what the birds sing and the brook, and talk with the flowers, and see faces in the sky, and hear music in the wind, I won't mind being a child, even if people call me queer."

"You shall understand many lovely things and be able to put them into tales and songs that all will read and sing and thank you for," said Moonbeam, a sweet, thoughtful elf, who stole quietly about, and was always singing like a soft wind.

"Oh, that is what I always wanted to do," cried Eva, "for I love my song-books best, and never find new ones enough. Show me more, dear elves, so that I can have many fine tales to tell when I am old enough to write."

"Come, then, and see our sweetest sight. We cannot show it to every one, but your eyes will be able to see through the veil, and you will understand the meaning of our flower-heaven."

So Moonlight led her away from all the rest, along a little winding path that went higher and higher till they stood on a hilltop.

"Look up and follow me," said the elf, and touching Eva's shoulders with her wand, a pair of wings shot out, and away she floated after her guide toward what looked like a white cloud sailing in the blue sky.

When they alighted, a soft mist was round them, and through it Eva saw a golden glimmer like sunshine.

"Look, but do not speak," said Moonlight, beckoning her along.

Soon the mist passed away and nothing but a thin veil of gossamer like a silken cobweb hung between them and the world beyond. "Can you see through it?" whispered the elf anxiously.

Eva nodded, and then forgot everything to look with all her eyes into a lovely land of flowers; for the walls were of white lilies, the trees were rose-trees, the ground blue violets, and the birds the little yellow canary-plant, whose blossoms are like birds on the wing. Columbines sounded their red horns, and the air was filled with delicate voices, unlike any ever heard before, because it was the sweet breath of flowers set to music.

But what surprised Eva most was the sight of a common dandelion, a tuft of clover, a faded mignonette-plant, with several other humble flowers, set in a little plot by themselves as if newly come, and about them gathered a crowd of beautiful spirits, so bright, so small, so perfect that Eva could hardly see them, and winked as if dazzled by the sunshine of this garden among the clouds.

"Who are they? and why do they care for those poor flowers?" whispered Eva, forgetting that she must not speak.

Before Moonlight could answer, all grew dim for a moment, as if a cold breath had passed beyond the curtain and chilled the delicate world within.

"Hush! mortal voices must not be heard here," answered the elf with a warning look.

"These lovely creatures are the spirits of flowers who did some good deed when they bloomed on earth, and their reward is to live here forever where there is no frost, no rain, no stormy wind to hurt them. Those poor plants have just come, for their work is done, and their souls will soon be set free from the shapes that hold them. You will see how beautiful they have made themselves when out of the common flowers come souls like the perfect ones who are welcoming them.

"That dandelion lived in the room of a poor little sick girl who had no other toy, no other playmate. She watched and loved it as she lay on her bed, for she was never well, and the good flower, instead of fading without sunshine in that dreary room, bloomed its best, till it shone like a little sun. The child died with it in her hand, and when she no longer needed it, we saved it from being thrown away and brought it here to live forever.

"The clover grew in a prison-yard, and a bad boy shut up there watched it as the only green thing that made him think of the fields at home where his mother was waiting and hoping he would come back to her. Clover did her best to keep good thoughts in his mind and he loved her, and tried to repent, and when he was told he might go, he meant to take his flower with him but forgot it in his hurry to get home. We did not forget, for the wind that goes everywhere had told us the little story, and we brought brave Clover out of prison to this flower-heaven.

"Mignonette lived in a splendid garden, but no one minded her, for she is only a little brown thing and hid in a corner, happy with her share of sunshine and rain, and her daily task of blossoming green and strong. People admired the other fine flowers and praised their perfume, never knowing that the sweetest breath of all came from the nook where Mignonette modestly hid behind the roses. No one ever praised her, or came to watch her, and the gardener took no care of her. But the bees found her out and came every day to sip her sweet honey, the butterflies loved her better than the proud roses, and the wind always stopped for a kiss as it flew by. When autumn came and all the other plants were done blossoming, and stood bare and faded, there was modest Mignonette still green and fresh, still with a blossom or two, and still smiling contentedly with a bosom full of ripened seeds, — her summer work well done, her happy heart ready for the winter sleep.

"But we said, 'No frost shall touch our brave flower; she shall not be neglected another year, but come to live loved and honored in the eternal summer that shines here.' Now look."

Eva brushed away the tears that had filled her eyes as she listened to these little histories, and looking eagerly, saw how from the dandelion, set free by the spells the spirits sang, there rose, light as down, a little golden soul, in the delicate shape the others wore. One in pale rose came from the clover, and a third in soft green with dusky wings; but a bright face flew out of the mignonette. Then the others took hands and floated round the newcomers in an airy dance, singing so joyfully that Eva clapped her hands crying, "Happy souls! I will go home and try to be as good as they were; then I may be as happy when I go away to my heaven."

The sound of her voice made all dark, and she would have been frightened if the elf had not taken her hand and led her back to the edge of the cloud, saying as they flew down to Fairyland — "See, the sun is setting; we must take you home before this midsummer day ends, and with it our power to make ourselves known."

Eva had so much to tell that she was ready to go; but a new surprise waited for her, and she saw a fairy spectacle as she came again before the palace.

Banners of gay tulip-leaves were blowing in the wind from the lances of reeds held by a troop of elves mounted on mice; a car made of a curled green leaf with checkerberry wheels and cushions of pink mushrooms stood ready for her, and Trip as maid of honor helped her in. Lady elves on butterflies flew behind, and the Queen's trumpeters marched before making music on their horns. All the people of Elf-

Eva's Visit to Fairyland

land lined the way, throwing flowers, waving their hands, and calling, "Farewell, little Eva! Come again! Do not forget us!" till she was out of sight.

"How sweet and kind you are to me. What can I do to thank you?" said Eva to Trip, who sat beside her as they rolled along, — a gay and lovely sight, if any but fairy eyes could have seen it.

"Remember all you have seen and heard. Love the good and beautiful things you will find everywhere, and be always a happy child at heart," answered Trip with a kiss.

Before Eva could speak, the sun set and in a moment every elf was invisible, all the pretty show was gone, and the child stood alone by the brook. But she never forgot her visit to Fairyland, and as she grew up, she seemed to be a sort of elf herself, happy, gay, and good, with the power of making every one love her as she went singing and smiling through the world. She wrote songs that people loved to sing, told tales children delighted to read, and found so much wisdom, beauty, and music everywhere, that it was very plain she understood the sweet language of bird and flower, wind and water, and remembered all the lessons the elves taught her.

THE FROST KING AND HOW THE FAIRIES CONQUERED HIM

THE Queen sat upon her throne, and all the fairies from the four kingdoms were gathered for a grand council. A very important question was to be decided, and the bravest, wisest elves were met to see what could be done. The Frost King made war upon the flowers; and it was a great grief to Queen Blossom and her subjects to see their darlings die year after year, instead of enjoying one long summer, as they might have done but for him. She had sent messengers with splendid gifts, and had begged him to stop this dreadful war, which made autumn so sad and left the fields strewn with dead flowers. But he sent back the gifts, sternly refused her prayers, and went on with his cruel work; because he was a tyrant, and loved to destroy innocent things.

"My subjects, we will try once more," said the Queen, "if any one can propose a plan that will touch his hard heart and make him kind to the dear flowers."

Then there was a great rustling of wings and murmuring of voices; for all the elves were much excited, and each wanted to propose something. The Queen listened, but none of the plans seemed wise, and she was sadly perplexed, when her favorite maid of honor, the lovely Star, came and knelt before her, saying, while her face shone and her voice trembled with the earnestness of her words, "Dear Queen, let me go alone to the Frost King and try what love will do. We have sent presents and prayers by messengers who feared and hated him, and he would not receive them; but we have not tried to make him love us, nor shown him how beautiful his land might be, by patiently changing that dreary place, and teaching his people to plant flowers, not to kill them. I am not afraid; let me go and try my plan, for love is very powerful, and I know he has a heart if we can only find it."

"You may go, dear Star," answered the Queen, "and see if you can conquer him. But if any harm happens to you, we will come with our whole army and fight this cruel King till he is conquered."

At these brave words all the elves cheered, and General Sun, the great warrior, waved his sword as if longing to go to battle at once. They gathered about Star, — some to praise and caress her, some to warn her of the dangers of her task, others to tell her the way, and every one to wish her success; for fairies are gentle little creatures, and believe heartily in the power of love.

Star wished to go at once; so they wrapped her in a warm cloak of down from a swan's breast, gave her a bag of the seeds of all their sweetest flowers, and with kisses and tears went to the gates of Fairyland to say good-by.

Smiling bravely she flew away toward the North, where the frost spirits lived. Soon the wind grew cold, the sunshine faded, and snow began to fall, making Star shiver under her soft cloak. Presently she saw the King's palace. Pillars of ice held up the roof fringed with icicles, which would have sparkled splendidly if there had been any sun. But all was dark and cold, and not a green leaf rustled, or bird sang in the wide plains, white with snow, that stretched as far as the eye could see. Before the doors stood the guard, frozen to their places, who lifted their sharp spears and let Star go in when she said she was a messenger from the Queen.

Walls of ice carved with strange figures were round her, long icicles hung from the roof, and carpets of snow covered the floor. On a throne hung with gray mist sat the King; a crown of crystals was on his white hair, and his mantle was covered with silver frost-work. His eyes were cold, his face stern, and a smile never moved his hard lips. He frowned as he saw the fairy, and drew his cloak closer, as if afraid the light of her bright face might soften his heart.

Then Star told her errand, and in her gentle voice begged him to be kind. She described the sorrow of both elves and children when his frost killed all the flowers; she painted a bright picture of a world where it was always summer, and asked him to let her show how lovely flowers made any spot, by planting some in his bleak fields.

But he only scowled and ordered her away, saying harshly, "I will do as I please; and if your Queen does not leave me in peace, I will go to war and freeze every fairy to death."

Star tried to say more, but he was so angry that he called his people and bid them shut her up till she would own that he was right and promise to let him kill all the flowers he liked.

"I never will do that," said Star, as the Frost people led her away to a dark little cell, and left her alone.

She was cold and tired and very sad because the King would not listen to her, but her heart was brave, and instead of crying she began to sing. Soon the light of her own eyes, that shone like stars, made a little glimmer in the dark, and she saw that the floor of her cell was of earth; and presently she heard the tinkle of water as it dripped drop by drop down from the snow above. Then she smiled, so that it seemed as if a ray of light had crept in.

"Here is earth and water; I will make the sunshine, and soon by my fairy power I will have a garden even in Frostland." As she spoke, she pulled out the seeds and fell to work, still singing, still smiling, still sure that in time she would do the hard task she had set herself. First she gathered the drops in her warm hands and moistened the hard earth; then she loosened it and planted her seeds along the walls; and then, sitting in the middle of the narrow room, she waved her wand and chanted the fairy spell that works the pretty miracle of turning seeds to flowers.

"Sleep, little seed,
Deep in your bed,
While winter snow
Lies overhead.
Wake, little sprout,
And drink the rain,
Till sunshine calls
You to rise again.

> Strike deep, young root,
> In the earth below;
> Unfold, pale leaves,
> Begin to grow.
> Baby bud, dance
> In the warm sun;
> Bloom, sweet rose,
> Life has begun."

As she sung, the light grew stronger, the air warmer, and the drops fell like dew, till up came rows of little green vines and plants, growing like the magic beanstalk all over the walls and all round the room, making the once dark place look like a bower. Moss spread like a carpet underfoot, and a silvery white mushroom sprung up under Star, as if she were the queen of this pretty place.

Soon the Frost spirits heard the music and went to see who dared sing in that gloomy prison. They were much surprised when they peeped, to see that instead of dying in her cell, the fairy had made it beautiful, and sat there singing while her flowers bloomed in spite of all their power.

They hurried to the King and bade him come and see. He went, and when he saw the lovely place, he could not spoil it till he had watched Star at her work, and tried to see what magic did such wonders. For now the dark walls were hung with morning-glories, ringing their many-colored bells, the floor was green with soft moss, the water-drops made music as they fell, and rows of flowers nodded from their beds as if talking together in a sweet language of their own. Star sat on her throne still singing and smiling, till the once dark place was as bright as if a little sun shone there.

"I am strong, but I cannot do that," said the King. "I love power, and perhaps if I watch, I shall learn some of her magic skill to use as I please. I will let her live, but keep her a prisoner, and do as I please about killing other flowers."

So he left her there, and often stole down to peep, and wonder at her cheerfulness and courage; for she never complained or cried, though she longed for home, and found it very hard to be brave and patient.

Meantime the Queen waited and waited for Star to come, and when a long time passed, she sent a messenger to learn where she was. He brought back the sad tidings that she was a prisoner, and the King would not let her go. Then there was great weeping and wailing in Fairyland, for every one loved gentle Star. They feared she would be frozen to death if they left her in the cruel King's power, and resolved to go to war as he would not set her free.

General Sun ordered out the army, and there was a great blowing of trumpets, beating of drums, and flying of flags as the little soldiers came marching from the four quarters of the kingdom. The earth elves were on foot, in green suits, with acorn cups for helmets and spear grass for lances. The water sprites were in blue armor made of dragon-fly scales, and they drew shells full of tiny bubbles that were shot like cannon-balls, upsetting their small enemies by the dozen. The fire imps wore red, and carried torches to burn, and little guns to shoot bullets of brimstone from, which killed by their dreadful smell. The air spirits were the finest of all; for they were in golden armor, and carried arrows of light, which they shot from tiny rainbows. These came first, and General Sun was splendid to behold as he led them shining and flashing before the Queen, whose great banner of purple and gold streamed over their heads, while the trumpets blew, the people cheered, and the elfin soldiers marched bravely away to fight the Frost King and bring Star home.

The Queen followed in her chariot drawn by white butterflies, with her maids, and her body guard of the tallest elves in Fairyland. They lived in the pine-trees, and were fine strong fellows, with little cones on their heads, pine needles for swords, and the handsome russet scales for chain armor. Their shields were of sweet-smelling gum, like amber; but no one could approach the Queen when they made a wall about her, for whoever touched these shields stuck fast, and were killed with the sharp swords.

Away streamed the army like a wandering rainbow, and by and by reached the land of frost and snow. The King had been warned that they were coming, and made ready by building a fort of ice, laying in piles of snow-balls, and arming his subjects with sharp icicles. All the cold winds that blow wailed like bag-pipes, hailstones drummed on the frozen ground, and banners of mist floated over the towers of the palace. General Fog, in a suit of silver, stood ready to meet the enemy, with an army of snow men behind him, and the Frost King looked down from the walls to direct the fight.

On came the fairy folk, making the icy world sparkle so brilliantly with their light that the King was half-blinded and hid his eyes. The elves shivered as the cold wind touched them, but courage kept them warm, and the Queen, well wrapped in down, stood up in her chariot, boldly demanding Star at the hands of the King.

"I will not give her up," he answered, scowling like a thunder-cloud, though in his heart he wondered more and more how the brave fairy had lived so long away from such lovely friends as these.

"Then I proclaim war upon your country; and if Star is dead, we will show no mercy. Sound the trumpets and set on!" cried the Queen, waving her hand to the General, while every sword flashed out, and an elfin cheer rung like music in the air.

Ordering the rest to halt, General Sun led the air spirits to battle first, well knowing that nothing could stand long before a charge of that brilliant troop. General Fog did his best, but was driven back against his will; for his snow men melted away as the arrows of light struck them, and he could not stand before the other general, whose shield was a golden sun, without feeling himself dissolve like mist at noon.

They were forced to take refuge in the fort, where the King himself was ordering showers of snow-balls to be shot among the fairy troops. Many were wounded, and carried from the field to the tent where the Queen and her maids tended them, and by their soft magic soon made them fit to fight again.

"Now, a grand attack. Bring up the sappers and miners, Captain Rock. Major Flash, surround the walls and melt them as fast as possible, while the archers shall go on shooting," commanded General Sun.

Then a company of moles began to dig under the fort; the fire imps banged away at the walls with their cannon, and held their flaming torches close till the blocks of ice began to melt; the air spirits flew high above and shot their golden arrows down at the Frost people, who fled away to hide in the darkest corners, dazzled and daunted by these brave and brilliant enemies.

It was a hard battle, and the fairies were obliged to rest, after killing General Fog, destroying the fort, and forcing the King to take refuge in the palace. Among the prisoners taken was one who told them where Star was, and all she had done in her little cell. Then they rejoiced, and the Queen said, "Let us follow her example, for these prisoners say the King is changed since she came; that he goes to peep at her lovely bower, and does not spoil it, but talks kindly to her, and seems as if his hard heart might be melting a little. We will not fight any more, but try Star's gentle way, and besiege the King till he surrenders; so we shall win a friend, not kill an enemy."

"We will; we will!" cried all the elves; for they did not love to fight, though brave as little lions to defend their country and their Queen. They all took counsel together, and the Frost people were surprised next day to see the army busily at work making a great garden round the palace instead of trying to destroy it. Creeping to the holes in the walls they watched what went on, and wondered more and more; for the elves worked hard, and their magic helped them to do in a day what it would have taken years for mortals to do.

First the moles dug up the ground, then the Queen's guard sowed pine seeds, and in an hour a green wall fenced in the garden where the earth fairies planted seeds of all the flowers that grow. The fire imps warmed the air, and drove away every chilly wind, every gray cloud or flake of snow that dared come near this enchanted spot. The water sprites gathered drops from the melting ice palace and watered the budding beds, after the imps had taken the chill off, while the air spirits made sunshine overhead by flying to and fro with tireless wings, till a golden curtain was woven that shut out the cold sky and made summer for the flowers.

The Queen and her maids helped, for they fashioned birds, bees, and butterflies with magic skill, and gave them life to sing, buzz, and flutter in the new world, growing so fast where once all was bare and cold and dark.

Slowly the ice palace melted; for warm airs stole through the pines, and soon the walls were thin as glass, the towers vanished like frost-work in the sun, and block after block flowed away in little rills as if glad to escape from prison. The King and his subjects felt that they were conquered; for the ice seemed to melt from them also, and their hearts began to beat, their cold faces to soften as if they wanted to smile if they knew how, and they loved to watch and wonder at the sweet miracles the elves were working all about them.

The King tried not to give up, for he was very proud, and had ruled so long it was hard to submit; but his power was gone, his palace crumbling about him, his people longing to join the enemy, and there was nothing for him to do but lay down his crown or fly away to the far North and live with the bears and icebergs in that frozen world. He would have done this but for Star. All the while the battle and the siege were going on, she lived in her little cell, knowing nothing about it, but hoping and waiting, sure that help would come. Every time the King visited her he seemed kinder, and liked more and more to listen to her songs or the stories she told him of life in Fairyland, and the joy of being merciful. So she knew that the seeds she sowed in his heart were beginning to grow like those planted in the cell, and she watched over them as carefully.

One day her loveliest roses bloomed, and she was singing for joy as the pink flowers filled the cell with their sweet breath, when the King came hurrying down to her and falling at her feet begged her to save his life. She wondered what he meant, and he told her of the battle, and how the elves were conquering him by love; for the palace was nearly gone, a great garden lay blossoming all about it, and he had nowhere to go unless she would be his friend and ask her people to forgive and pity him.

Then Star felt that she had done her task, and laying her hands on his white head, she melted the last frost from his old heart by saying in her tender voice, "Do not fear my people; they will welcome you and give you a home if you will promise to hurt no more flowers, but always be as gentle as you are now. Come with me, and let us teach you how beautiful sunshine and love and happy work can make you."

The King promised, and Star led him up to the light again, where his people waited to know what was to become of them.

"Follow me, follow me, and do not be afraid," called Star, dancing before them, — so glad to be free that she longed to fly away. Everything was changed; for as they came up from the cell, the ruins of the palace melted into a quiet lake, and under the archway of the pines they passed into a new and lovely world of sunshine, flowers, and happy elves. A great cry went up when Star was seen leading the King, with his few subjects behind him, and every one flew to welcome the dear fairy and the captives she brought.

"I am your prisoner, and I submit, for I have no kingdom now," said the King, as he bowed before the Queen.

"These are the only chains you shall wear, and *this* is your new kingdom," answered the Queen, as her maids hung wreaths of flowers on the King's arms and put a green crown on his head, while all the fairies gathered round to welcome him to the lovely garden where he was to reign beloved and happy, with no frost to spoil the long summer he had learned to love.

There was a great feast that day, and then the elfin army marched home again, well pleased with the battle they had fought, though all said that it was Star who had conquered the Frost-King.

LILYBELL AND THISTLEDOWN, OR THE FAIRY SLEEPING BEAUTY

ONCE upon a time two little fairies went out into the world to seek their fortune. Thistledown wore a green suit, a purple cloak, a gay feather in his cap, and was as handsome an elf as one could wish to see. But he was not loved in Fairyland; for, like the flower whose name and colors he wore, many faults like sharp prickles were hidden under his fine clothes. He was idle, selfish, and cruel, and cared for nothing but his own pleasure and comfort, as we shall see.

His little friend Lilybell was very different, for she was so kind and good every one loved her. She spent her time trying to undo the mischief naughty Thistle did, and that was why she followed him now, because she was afraid he would get into trouble and need some one to help him.

Side by side they flew over hill and dale till they came to a pleasant garden.

"I am tired and hungry," said Thistle; "let us rest here and see what fun is going on."

"Now, dear Thistle, be kind and gentle, and make friends among these flowers. See how they spread their leaves for our beds, and offer us their honey to eat, and their dew to bathe in. It would be very wrong to treat them badly after such a welcome as this," answered Lilybell, as she lay down to sleep in the deep cup of one of her own flowers, as if in a little bed hung with white curtains.

Thistle laughed and flew off to find the tulips, for he liked splendid flowers and lived like a king. First he robbed the violets of their honey, and shook the blue-bells roughly to get all their dew for his bath. Then he ruffled many leaves before his bed suited him, and after a short nap was up and away having what he called fun. He chased the butterflies and hurt them with the sharp thorn he carried for a sword; he broke the cobwebs laid to bleach on the grass for fairy cloth; he pushed the little birds out of the nest and killed them; he stole pollen from the busy bees, and laughed to see them patiently begin to fill their little bags again. At last he came to a lovely rose-tree with one open flower and a little bud.

"Why are you so slow about blooming, baby rose? You are too old to be rocked in your green cradle any longer. Come out and play with me," said Thistle, as he perched on the tree ready for more mischief.

"No, my little bud is not strong enough to meet the sun and air yet," answered the rose-mother, bending over her baby, while all her red leaves trembled with fear, for the wind had told her the harm this cruel fairy had been doing in the garden.

"You silly flower, to wait so long. See how quickly I will make the ugly green bud a pretty pink rose," cried Thistle, as he pulled open the folded bud so rudely that the little leaves fell all broken on the ground.

"It was my first and only one, and I was so fond and proud of it! Now you have killed it, cruel fairy, and I am all alone," sobbed the mother, while her tears fell like rain on the poor bud fading in the hot sun.

Thistle was ashamed of himself, but he would not say he was sorry, and flew away to hunt a white moth, till clouds began to gather and a shower came on. Then he hurried back to the tulips for shelter, sure they would take him in because he had praised their gay colors, and they were vain flowers. But when he came all wet and cold begging to be covered, they laughed and shook their broad leaves till the drops fell on him faster than the rain and beat him down.

"Go away, naughty fairy! we know you now,

and won't let you in, for you bring trouble wherever you go. You needn't come to us for a new cloak when the shower has spoilt that one," they cried.

"I don't care, the daisies will be glad to take pity on so splendid an elf as I am," said Thistle, as he flew down to the humble flowers in the grass.

But all the rosy leaves were tightly closed and he knocked in vain, for the daisies had heard of his pranks, and would not risk spoiling their seeds by opening to such a naughty fellow.

He tried the buttercups and dandelions, the violets and mignonette, the lilies and the honeysuckles, but all shut their doors against him and told him to go away.

"Now I have no friends and I must die of cold. If I had only minded Lilybell, I might be safe and warm as she is somewhere," sighed Thistle, as he stood shivering in the rain.

"I have no little bud to shelter now, and you can come in here," said a soft voice above him; and looking up, Thistle saw that he was under the rose-tree where the dead bud hung broken on its stem.

Grieved and ashamed, the fairy gladly crept in among the warm red leaves, and the rose-mother held him close to her gentle bosom where no rain or chilly wind could reach him. But when she thought

Lilybell and Thistledown

he was asleep, she sighed so sadly over her lost baby that Thistle found no rest, and dreamed only sad dreams.

Soon the sun shone again and Lilybell came to find her friend; but he was ashamed to meet her and stole away. When the flowers told Lily all the harm Thistle had done, she was very sorrowful, and tried to comfort them. She cured the hurt birds and butterflies, helped the bees he had robbed, and watered the poor rose till more buds came to bloom on her stem. Then when all were well and happy again, she went to find Thistle, leaving the garden full of grateful friends.

Meantime, Thistle had been playing more pranks, and got into trouble. A kind bee invited him to dinner one day, and the fairy liked the pretty home in the hive; for the floors were of white wax, the walls of golden honey-comb, and the air sweet with the breath of flowers. It was a busy place; some got the food and stored it up in the little cells; some were the housemaids, and kept all exquisitely neat; some took care of the eggs and fed the young bees like good nurses; and others waited on the Queen.

"Will you stay and work with us? No one is idle here, and it is a happier life than playing all day," said Buzz, the friendly bee.

"I hate to work," answered lazy Thistle, and would not do anything at all.

Then they told him he must go; that made him angry, and he went to some of the bees whom he had made discontented by his fine tales of an idle life, and said to them, —

"Let us feast and be jolly; winter is far off and there is no need to work in the summer time. Come and make merry, while those busy fellows are away, and the nurses watching the babies in the cells."

Then he led the drones to the hive, like a band of robbers; first they fastened the Queen into her royal room, so she could do nothing but buzz angrily; next they drove the poor housekeepers away, and frightened the little bees into fits as they went rioting through the waxen halls, pulling down the honey-comb, and stealing the bee-bread carefully put away in the neat cells for winter time. They stayed as long as they dared, and flew off before the workers came home to find their pretty hive in ruins.

"That was fine fun," said Thistle, as he went to hide in a great forest where he thought the angry bees could not find him.

Here he soon made friends with a gay dragon-fly, and they had splendid games skimming over the lake or swinging on the ferns that grew about it. For a while Thistle was good, and might have had a happy time if he had not quarrelled with his friend about a little fish that the cruel elf pricked with his sword till it nearly died. Gauzy-wing thought that very cruel, and said he would tell the Brownies who ruled over everything in the wood.

"I'm not afraid," answered Thistle; "they can't hurt me."

But he *was* afraid, and as soon as the dragon-fly was asleep that night, he got an ugly spider to come and spin webs all round the poor thing till it could stir neither leg nor wing.

Then leaving it to starve, Thistle flew out of the wood, sure that the Brownies would not catch him.

But they did, for they knew all that happened in their kingdom; and when he stopped to rest in a wild morning-glory-bell, they sent word by the wind that he was to be kept a prisoner till they came. So the purple leaves closed round the sleeping fairy, and he woke to find himself held fast. Then he knew how poor Gauzy-wing felt, and wished he had not been so unkind. But it was too late, for soon the Brownies came, and tying his wings with a strong blade of grass said as they led him away, —

"You do so much harm we are going to keep you

a prisoner till you repent, for no one can live in this beautiful world unless he is kind and good. Here you will have time to think over your naughtiness, and learn to be a better elf."

So they shut him up in a great rock where there was no light but one little ray through a crack that let air into his narrow cell, and there poor Thistle sat alone longing to be free, and sobbing over all the pleasant things he had lost. By and by he stopped crying, and said to himself, —

"Perhaps if I am patient and cheerful, even in this dark place, the Brownies will let me out." So he began to sing, and the more he sang the better he felt, for the ray of sunshine seemed to grow brighter, the days shorter, and his sorrow easier to bear, because he was trying to take his punishment bravely and be good.

Lilybell was looking for him all this time, tracing him by the harm he did, and stopping to comfort those whom he hurt; so she never found him till she had helped the bees put the hive in order, set free poor Gauzy-wing, and nursed the hurt fish till it was well again. Then she went on looking for him, and wondering where he was. She never would have guessed if he had not sung so much, for the birds loved to hear him, and often perched on the rocks

Lilybell and Thistledown

to listen and learn the fairy songs. Columbines sprung up there in the sunshine and danced on their slender stems as they peeped in at him with rosy faces, while green moss went creeping up the sides of the rock as if eager to join in the music.

As Lilybell came to this pleasant place, she wondered if there was a fairy party going on, for the birds were singing, the flowers dancing, and the old rock looked very gay. When they saw her, the birds stopped, and the columbines stood so still that she heard a voice singing sadly, —

> "Bright shines the summer sun,
> Soft in the summer air,
> Gayly the wood-birds sing,
> Flowers are blooming fair.
> But deep in the dark, cold rock
> All alone must I dwell,
> Longing for you, dear friend,
> Lilybell, Lilybell!"

"Where are you?" cried the other fairy, flying up among the columbines; for she could see no opening in the rock, and wondered where the voice came from. No one replied, for Thistle did not hear her, so she sang her answer to his call, —

"Through sunshine and shower
I have looked for you long,
Guided by bird and flower,
And now by your song,
Thistledown! Thistledown!
O'er wood, hill, and dell
Hither to comfort you
Comes Lilybell."

Then through the narrow opening two arms were stretched out to her, and all the columbines danced for joy that Thistle was found.

Lilybell made her home there, and did all she could to cheer the poor prisoner, glad to see that he was sorry for his naughtiness, and really trying to be good. But he pined so to come out that she could not bear it, and said she would go and ask the Brownies what he could do to be free.

Thistle waited and waited, but she did not come back, and he cried and called so pitifully that the Brownies came at last and took him out, saying, —

"Lilybell is safe, but she is in a magic sleep, and will not wake till you bring us a golden wand from the earth elves, a cloak of sunshine from the air spirits, and a crown of diamonds from the water fairies. It is a hard task, for you have no friends to help you along. But if you love Lilybell enough to be patient, brave, and kind, you may succeed, and she will wake to reward you when you bring the fairy gifts."

As they said this, the Brownies led him to a green tent made of tall ferns, and inside on a bed of moss lay Lilybell fast asleep, like the Beauty in the dear old story.

"I will do it," said Thistle, and spreading the wings that had been idle so long, he was off like a humming-bird.

"Flowers know most about the earth elves, so I will ask them," he thought, and began to ask every clover and buttercup, wood-violet, and wayside dandelion that he met. But no one would answer him; all shrunk away and drew their curtains close, remembering his rough treatment before.

"I will go to the rose; I think she is a friend, for she forgave me, and took me in when the rest left me in the cold," said Thistle, much discouraged, and half afraid to ask anything of the flower he had hurt so much.

But when he came to the garden, the rose-mother welcomed him kindly, and proudly showed the family of little buds that now grew on her stem.

"I will trust and help you for Lilybell's sake," she said. "Look up, my darlings, and show the friend how rosy your little faces are growing; you need not be afraid now."

But the buds leaned closer to their mother, and would only peep at Thistle, for they remembered the little sister whom he had killed, and they feared him.

"Ah," he sadly thought, "if I had only been kind like Lily, they would all love and trust me, and be glad to help me. How beautiful goodness is! I must try to prove to them that I *am* sorry; then they will believe me, and show me how to find the crown."

So, at night when the flowers were asleep, he watered them; sung lullabies to the restless young birds, and tucked the butterflies up under the leaves where no dew could spoil their lovely wings. He rocked the baby-buds to sleep when they grew impatient before it was time to blossom; he kept grubs from harming the delicate leaves of the flowers, and brought cool winds to refresh them when the sun was hot.

The rose was always good to him, and when the other plants wondered who did so many kind things, she said to them, —

"It is Thistle, and he is so changed I am sure we

may trust him. He hides by day for no one is friendly, but by night he works or sits alone, and sobs and sighs so sadly I cannot sleep for pity."

Then they all answered, "We will love and help him for Lilybell's sake."

So they called him to come and be friends, and he was very happy to be forgiven. But he did not forget his task, and when he told them what it was, they called Downy-back, the mole, and bid him show Thistle where the earth elves lived. Thanking the kind flowers, Thistle followed the mole deep into the ground, along the road he knew so well, till they saw a light before them.

"There they are; now you can go on alone, and good luck to you," said Downy-back, as he scampered away, — for he liked the dark best.

Thistle came to a great hall made of jewels that shone like the sun, and here many spirits were dancing like fire-flies to the music of silver bells.

One of these came and asked why he was there, and when he told her, Sparkle said, "You must work for us if you want to earn the golden wand."

"What must I do?" asked Thistle.

"Many things," answered Sparkle; "some of us watch over the roots of the flowers and keep them warm and safe; others gather drops and make springs that gush up among the rocks, where people drink the fresh water and are glad; others dig for jewels, make good-luck pennies, and help miners find gold and silver hidden in dark places. Can you be happy here, and do all these things faithfully?"

"Yes, for love of Lily I can do anything," said Thistle bravely, and fell to work at once with all his heart.

It was hard and dull for the gay fairy, who loved light and air, to live in the earth like a mole; and often he was very sad and tired, and longed to fly away to rest. But he never did, and at last Sparkle said, "You have done enough. Here is the golden wand, and as many jewels as you like."

But Thistle cared only for the wand, and hurried up to the sunshine as fast as he could climb, eager to show the Brownies how well he had kept his word.

They were very glad to see him back and told him to rest a little. But he could not wait, and with a look at Lily, still fast asleep, he flew away to find the air spirits.

No one seemed to know where they lived, and Thistle was in despair till he remembered hearing Buzz speak of them when he first met him.

"I dare not go to the hive, for the bees might

Lilybell and Thistledown 83

kill me, I did so much harm. Perhaps if I first show them I am sorry, they will forgive me as the flowers did," he said.

So he went into a field of clover and worked busily till he had filled two blue-bells full of the sweetest honey. These he left at the door of the hive when no one saw him, and then hid in the apple-tree close by.

The bees were much pleased and surprised; for every day two little blue jars stood at the door, full of honey so fresh and sweet that it was kept for the Queen and the royal babies.

"It is some good elf, who knows how much trouble we have had this summer, and wants to help us fill our cells before the frost comes. If we catch the kind fellow, we will thank him well," said the bees gratefully.

"Ah, ha! we shall be friends again, I think, if I keep on," laughed Thistle, much cheered as he sat among the leaves.

After this he not only left the pretty honey-pots, but flew far and wide for all the flowering herbs bees love to suck, and nearly broke his back lugging berries from the wood, or great bags of pollen for their bread, till he was as dusty as a little miller. He helped the ants with their heavy loads, the field-mice with their small harvesting, and chased flies from the patient cows feeding in the fields. No one saw him, but all loved "Nimble Nobody" as they called the invisible friend who did so many kindly things.

At last they caught him, as he was wrapping a lizard who had chills in a warm mullein-leaf blanket.

"Why, it is naughty Thistle!" cried the bees, ready to sting him to death.

"No, no," chirped an old cricket, who had kept the secret. "It is the good fellow who has done so much to make us all happy and comfortable. Put up your stings and shake hands, before he flies away to hide from you again."

The bees could hardly believe this at first, but finding it true were glad to make up the quarrel and be friends. When they heard what Thistle wanted, they consented at once, and sent Buzz to show him the way to Cloudland, where the air spirits lived.

It seemed a lovely place, for the sky was gold and purple overhead, silver mist hung like curtains from the rainbow arches, and white clouds were piled up like downy cushions for the spirits to sleep on. But they were very busy flying to and fro like motes in a sunbeam, some polishing the stars that they might shine well at night, some drawing up water from rivers and lakes, to shower it down again in rain or dew; others sent messages by the winds that kept coming and going like telegraph-boys, with news from all parts of the world; and others were weaving light into a shining stuff to hang on dark walls, wrap about budding plants, and clothe all spirits of the airy world.

"These are the ones I want," said Thistle, and asked for the mantle of sunshine.

"You must earn it first, and help us work," answered the weavers.

Thistle willingly went with them and shared their lovely tasks; but most of all he liked to shake sweet dreams from the dreamland tree down upon little people in their beds, to send strong, bright rays suddenly into dark rooms, dancing on the walls and cheering sick or sad eyes. Sometimes he went riding to the earth on a raindrop, like a little water-cart man, and sprinkled the dusty road or gave some thirsty plant a good drink. He helped the winds carry messages, and blow flower-seeds into lonely places to spring and blossom there, a pleasant surprise for all who might find them.

It was a busy and a happy life, and he liked it; for

fairies love light, air, and motion, and he was learning to live for good and helpful things. Sooner than he expected the golden cloak was won, and he shot like a falling star to the forest with his prize.

"One more trial and she will wake," said the Brownies, well pleased.

"This I shall not like, for I am not a water elf, but I'll do my best," answered Thistle, and roamed away into the wood, following a brook till he came to the lake where he used to play with Gauzy-wing. As he stood wondering how to find the nixies, he heard a faint cry for help, and presently found a little frog with a broken leg, lying on the moss.

"I tried to jump too far, when a cruel child was going to tread on me, and fell among the stones; I long for the water, but can drag myself no farther," sighed the frog, his bright eyes dim with pain.

Thistle did not like to touch the cold thing, but remembering his own unkindness to the dragon-fly, he helped the poor froggie to a fallen oak-leaf, and then tugged it by its stout stem to the waterside where he could bathe the hurt leg and bring cool draughts in an acorn cup.

"Alas! I cannot swim, and I am very tired of this bed," cried poor Hop after a day or two, during which Thistle fed and nursed him tenderly.

"I'll pull a lily-pad to the shore, and when you are on it, we can sail about wherever we please, without tiring you," and away went the elf to find the green boat.

After that they floated all day, and anchored at night, and Hop got well so fast that soon he could dive off and paddle a bit with his hands, or float, using his well leg to steer with. Thistle had talked about the water sprites, but Hop was rather a dull fellow, and lived in the mud, so he could tell him nothing. One day, however, a little fish popped up his head and said, —

"I know, and for kind Lilybell's sake I'll show you where they live."

Then Thistle left grateful Hop to his family, and folding his wings plunged into the lake after the silvery fish, who darted deeper and deeper till they stood in a curious palace made of rosy coral at the bottom of the sea. Gay shells made the floors and ornamented the walls. Lovely sea-weeds grew from the white sand, and heaps of pearls lay everywhere. The water sprites in their blue robes floated here and there, or slept in beds of foam, rocked by the motion of the waves.

They gathered round the stranger, bringing all sorts of treasures for him. But he did not care for these, and told them what he wanted. Then little Pearl, the gentlest of the sprites, said:

"You must help the coral-workers till the branches of their tree reach the air; because we want a new island, and that is the way we begin them. It is very dull work, but we cannot give you the crown till that is done."

Thistle was ready to begin at once, and hastened away to the coral-tree, where hundreds of little creatures were building cell upon cell, till the white tree rose tall and wide, spreading through the blue water. It *was* very dull, and the poor fairy never could lose his fear of the strange monsters that swam to and fro, staring at him with big eyes, or opening their great mouths as if to swallow him. There was no sun, — only a dim light, and the sky seemed full of storm, when the waves rolled overhead, and wrecks came floating down. The sea-flowers had no sweetness; the only birds were flying-fish and Mother Carey's chickens, as the stormy petrels are called. Thistle pined for light and air, but kept patiently at work, and his only pleasure was now and then to float with Pearl on the waves that rippled to the shore, and get a breath of warm air from the lovely earth he longed to see again.

At last the great tree rose above the sea, and the

long task was done; for now the waves would wash weeds over the branches, gulls would bring earth and sticks to make their nests, and by and by an island would be formed where men might land or wild birds live in peace.

"Now you can go. Here is the crown of water-drops, changed to diamonds, that will always lie cool and bright on your Lily's head. Good-by, good-by," said Pearl, as she gave the reward and waved her hand to Thistle, who shook the foam off his wings and flew away in the sunshine, like a happy butterfly just out of its cell.

When he came to the wood, the Brownies hastened to meet him, and he saw that they had made the place beautiful with wreaths from tree to tree; birds were singing their sweetest on every bough; the brook was laughing as it hurried by to tell the good news wherever it went; and the flowers, all in their best, were dancing with impatience to welcome him home.

Lilybell lay with the cloak of sunshine folded round her, and the golden wand in her hand, waiting for the crown and the kiss that should wake her from this long sleep. Thistle gave them both; and when her eyes opened and she stretched out her arms to him, he was the happiest fairy in the world.

The Brownies told all he had done, and how at last he had learned to be gentle, true, and brave, after many trials and troubles.

"You shall have the crown, for you have worked so hard you deserve it, and I will have a wreath of flowers," said Lily, so glad and proud she cared for nothing else.

"Keep your crown, for here are friends coming to bring Thistle his rewards," said the Brownies, as they pointed to a troop of earth spirits rising from among the mossy roots of an old tree. Sparkle brought a golden wand like the one he had earned for Lily, and while she was giving it, down through the air came the sky spirits, with the mantle of sunshine as their gift. Hardly had they folded it round happy Thistle, when the sound of music, like drops falling in time and tune, was heard, and along the brook in their boats of rosy shells came the water spirits with the crown.

As they put it on his head, all took hands and danced about the two elves, shouting in their soft voices, "Thistledown and Lilybell! Long live our King and Queen!"

THE CANDY COUNTRY

"I SHALL take mamma's red sun-umbrella, it is so warm, and none of the children at school will have one like it," said Lily, one day, as she went through the hall.

"The wind is very high; I'm afraid you'll be blown away if you carry that big thing," called Nurse from the window, as the red umbrella went bobbing down the garden walk with a small girl under it.

"I wish it would; I always wanted to go up in a balloon," answered Lily, as she struggled out of the gate.

She got on very well till she came to the bridge and stopped to look over the railing at the water running by so fast, and the turtles sunning themselves on the rocks. Lily was fond of throwing stones at them; it was so funny to watch them tumble, heels over head, splash into the water. Now, when she saw three big fellows close by, she stooped for a stone, and just at that minute a gale of wind nearly took the umbrella out of her hand. She clutched it fast; and away she went like a thistledown, right up in the air, over river and hill, houses and trees, faster and faster, till her head spun round, her breath was all gone, and she had to let go. The dear red umbrella flew away like a leaf; and Lily fell down, down, till she went crash into a tree which grew in such a curious place that she forgot her fright as she sat looking about her, wondering what part of the world it could be.

The tree looked as if made of glass or colored sugar; for she could see through the red cherries, the green leaves, and the brown branches. An agreeable smell met her nose; and she said at once, as any child would, "I smell candy!" She picked a cherry and ate it. Oh, how good it was! — all sugar and no stone. The next discovery was such a delightful one that she nearly fell off her perch; for by touching her tongue here and there, she found that the whole tree was made of candy. Think what fun to sit and break off twigs of barley sugar, candied cherries, and leaves that tasted like peppermint and sassafras!

Lily rocked and ate till she finished the top of the little tree; then she climbed down and strolled along, making more surprising and agreeable discoveries as she went.

What looked like snow under her feet was white sugar; the rocks were lumps of chocolate, the flowers of all colors and tastes; and every sort of fruit grew on these delightful trees. Little white houses soon appeared; and here lived the dainty candy-people, all made of the best sugar, and painted to look like real people. Dear little men and women, looking as if they had stepped off of wedding cakes and bonbons, went about in their gay sugar clothes, laughing and talking in the sweetest voices. Bits of babies rocked in open-work cradles, and sugar boys and girls played with sugar toys in the most natural way. Carriages rolled along the jujube streets, drawn by the red and yellow barley horses we all love so well; cows fed in the green fields, and sugar birds sang in the trees.

Lily listened, and in a moment she understood what the song said, —

> "Sweet! Sweet!
> Come, come and eat,
> Dear little girls
> With your yellow curls;
> For here you'll find
> Sweets to your mind.
> On every tree
> Sugar-plums you'll see;
> In every dell

Grows the caramel.
Over every wall
Gum-drops fall;
Molasses flows
Where our river goes.
Under your feet
Lies sugar sweet;
Over your head
Grow almonds red.
Our lily and rose
Are not for the nose;
Our flowers we pluck
To eat or suck.
And, oh! what bliss
When two friends kiss,
For they honey sip
From lip to lip!
And all you meet,
In house or street,
At work or play,
Sweethearts are they.
So, little dear,
Pray feel no fear;
Go where you will;
Eat, eat your fill.
Here is a feast

From west to east;
And you can say,
Ere you go away,
At last I stand
In dear Candy-land,
And no more can stuff;
For once I've enough.
Sweet! Sweet!
Tweet! Tweet!
Tweedle-dee!
Tweedle-dee!"

"That is the most interesting song I ever heard," said Lily, clapping her sticky hands and dancing along toward a fine palace of white cream candy, with pillars of striped peppermint stick, and a roof of frosting that made it look like the Milan Cathedral.

"I'll live here, and eat candy all day long, with no tiresome school or patchwork to spoil my fun," said Lily.

So she ran up the chocolate steps into the pretty rooms, where all the chairs and tables were of different colored candies, and the beds of spun sugar. A fountain of lemonade supplied drink; and floors of ice-cream that never melted kept people and things from sticking together, as they would have done had it been warm.

For a long while Lily was quite happy, going about tasting so many different kinds of sweeties, talking to the little people, who were very amiable, and finding out curious things about them and their country.

The babies were made of plain sugar, but the grown people had different flavors. The young ladies were flavored with violet, rose, and orange; the gentlemen were apt to have cordials of some sort inside of them, as she found when she ate one now and then slyly, and got her tongue bitten by the hot, strong taste as a punishment. The old people tasted of peppermint, clove, and such comfortable things, good for pain; but the old maids had lemon, hoarhound, flag-root, and all sorts of sour, bitter things in them, and did not get eaten much. Lily soon learned to know the characters of her new friends by a single taste, and some she never touched but once. The dear babies melted in her mouth, and the delicately flavored young ladies she was very fond of. Dr. Ginger was called to her more than once when so much candy made her teeth ache, and she found him a very hot-tempered little man; but he stopped the pain, so she was glad to see him.

A lime-drop boy and a little pink checkerberry girl were her favorite playmates; and they had fine times making mud-pies by scraping the chocolate rocks and mixing this dust with honey from the wells near by. These they could eat; and Lily thought this much better than throwing away the pies, as she had to do at home. They had candy-pulls very often, and made swings of long loops of molasses candy, and bird's-nests with almond eggs, out of which came birds who sang sweetly. They played foot-ball with big bull's-eyes, sailed in sugar boats on lakes of syrup, fished in rivers of molasses, and rode the barley horses all over the country.

Lily discovered that it never rained, but snowed white sugar. There was no sun, as it would have been too hot; but a large yellow lozenge made a nice moon, and red and white comfits were the stars.

The people all lived on sugar, and never quarrelled. No one was ill; and if any got broken, as sometimes happened with such brittle creatures, they just stuck the parts together and were all right again. The way they grew old was to get thinner and thinner till there was danger of their vanishing. Then the friends of the old person put him in a neat coffin, and carried him to the great golden urn which stood in their largest temple, always full of a certain fine syrup; and here he was dipped and dipped till he was stout and strong again, and went home to enjoy himself for a long time as good as new.

This was very interesting to Lily, and she went to many funerals. But the weddings were better still; for the lovely white brides were so sweet Lily longed to eat them. The feasts were delicious; and everybody went in their best clothes, and danced at the ball till they got so warm half-a-dozen would stick together and have to be taken to the ice-cream room to cool off. Then the little pair would drive away in a fine carriage with white horses to a new palace in some other part of the country, and Lily would have another pleasant place to visit.

But by and by, when she had seen everything, and eaten so much sweet stuff that at last she longed for plain bread and butter, she began to get cross, as children always do when they live on candy; and the little people wished she would go away, for they were afraid of her. No wonder, when she would catch up a dear sugar baby and eat him, or break some respectable old grandmamma all into bits because she reproved her for naughty ways. Lily calmly sat down on the biggest church, crushing it flat, and even tried to poke the moon out of the sky in a pet one day. The king ordered her to go home;

The Candy Country   99

but she said, "I won't!" and bit his head off, crown and all.

Such a wail went up at this awful deed that she ran away out of the city, fearing some one would put poison in her candy, since she had no other food.

"I suppose I shall get somewhere if I keep walking; and I can't starve, though I hate the sight of this horrid stuff," she said to herself, as she hurried over the mountains of Gibraltar Rock that divided the city of Saccharissa from the great desert of brown sugar that lay beyond.

Lily marched bravely on for a long time, and saw at last a great smoke in the sky, smelt a spicy smell, and felt a hot wind blowing toward her.

"I wonder if there are sugar savages here, roasting and eating some poor traveller like me," she said, thinking of Robinson Crusoe and other wanderers in strange lands.

She crept carefully along till she saw a settlement of little huts very like mushrooms, for they were made of cookies set on lumps of the brown sugar; and queer people, looking as if made of gingerbread, were working very busily round several stoves which seemed to bake at a great rate.

"I'll creep nearer and see what sort of people they are before I show myself," said Lily, going into a grove of spice-trees, and sitting down on a stone which proved to be the plummy sort of cake we used to call Brighton Rock.

Presently one of the tallest men came striding toward the trees with a pan, evidently after spice; and before she could run, he saw Lily.

"Hollo, what do you want?" he asked, staring at her with his black currant eyes, while he briskly picked the bark off a cinnamon-tree.

"I'm travelling, and would like to know what place this is, if you please," answered Lily, very politely, being a little frightened.

"Cake-land. Where do you come from?" asked the gingerbread man, in a crisp tone of voice.

"I was blown into the Candy country, and have been there a long time; but I got tired of it, and ran away to find something better."

"Sensible child!" and the man smiled till Lily thought his cheeks would crumble. "You'll get on better here with us Brownies than with the lazy Bonbons, who never work and are all for show. They won't own us, though we are all related through our grandparents Sugar and Molasses. We are busy folks; so they turn up their noses and don't speak when we meet at parties. Poor creatures, silly and sweet and unsubstantial! I pity 'em."

"Could I make you a visit? I'd like to see how you live, and what you do. I'm sure it must be interesting," said Lily, picking herself up after a tumble, having eaten nearly all the stone, she was so hungry.

"I know you will. Come on! I can talk while I work." And the funny gingerbread man trotted off toward his kitchen, full of pans, rolling-pins, and molasses jugs.

"Sit down. I shall be at leisure as soon as this batch is baked. There are still some wise people down below who like gingerbread, and I have my hands full," he said, dashing about, stirring, rolling out, and slapping the brown dough into pans, which he whisked into the oven and out again so fast that Lily knew there must be magic about it somewhere.

Every now and then he threw her a delicious cooky warm from the oven. She liked the queer fellow, and presently began to talk, being very curious about this country.

"What is your name, sir?"

"Ginger Snap."

Lily thought it a good one; for he was very quick, and she fancied he could be short and sharp if he liked.

"Where does all this cake go to?" she asked, after watching the other kitchens full of workers, who were all of different kinds of cake, and each set of cooks made its own sort.

"I'll show you by and by," answered Snap, beginning to pile up the heaps of gingerbread on a little car that ran along a track leading to some unknown storeroom, Lily thought.

"Don't you get tired of doing this all the time?"

"Yes; but I want to be promoted, and I never shall be till I've done my best, and won the prize here."

"Oh, tell me about it! What is the prize, and how are you promoted? Is this a cooking-school?"

"Yes; the prize for best gingerbread is a cake of condensed yeast. That puts a soul into me, and I begin to rise till I am able to go over the hills yonder into the blessed land of bread, and be one of the happy creatures who are always wholesome, always needed, and without which the world below would be in a bad way."

"Bless me! that is the queerest thing I've heard yet. But I don't wonder you want to go; I'm tired of sweets myself, and long for a good piece of bread, though I used to want cake and candy at home."

"Ah, my dear, you'll learn a good deal here; and you are lucky not to have got into the clutches of Giant Dyspepsia, who always gets people if they eat too much of such rubbish and scorn wholesome bread. I leave my ginger behind when I go, and get white and round and beautiful, as you will see. The Gingerbread family have never been as foolish as some of the other cakes. Wedding is the worst; such extravagance in the way of wine and spice and fruit I never saw, and such a mess to eat when it's done! I don't wonder people get sick; serves 'em right." And Snap flung down a pan with such a bang that it made Lily jump.

"Sponge cake isn't bad, is it? Mamma lets me eat it, but I like frosted pound better," she said, looking over to the next kitchen, where piles of that sort of cake were being iced.

"Poor stuff. No substance. Ladies' fingers will do for babies, but pound has too much butter ever to be healthy. Let it alone, and eat cookies or seed-cakes, my dear. Now, come along; I'm ready." And Snap trundled away his car-load at a great pace.

Lily ran behind to pick up whatever fell, and looked about her as she went, for this was certainly a very queer country. Lakes of eggs all beaten up, and hot springs of saleratus foamed here and there ready for use. The earth was brown sugar or ground spice; and the only fruits were raisins, dried currants, citron, and lemon peel. It was a very busy place; for every one cooked all the time, and never failed and never seemed tired, though they got so hot that they only wore sheets of paper for clothes. There were piles of it to put over the cake, so that it shouldn't burn; and they made cook's white caps and aprons of it, and looked very nice. A large clock made of a flat pancake, with cloves to mark the hours and two toothpicks for hands, showed them how long to bake things; and in one place an ice wall was built round a lake of butter, which they cut in lumps as they wanted it.

"Here we are. Now, stand away while I pitch 'em down," said Snap, stopping at last before a hole in the ground where a dumb-waiter hung ready, with a name over it.

There were many holes all round, and many waiters, each with its name; and Lily was amazed when she read "Weber," "Copeland," "Dooling," and others, which she knew very well.

Over Snap's place was the name "Newmarch;" and Lily said, "Why, that's where mamma gets her hard gingerbread, and Weber's is where we go for ice-cream. Do *you* make cake for them?"

"Yes, but no one knows it. It's one of the secrets of the trade. We cook for all the confectioners, and people think the good things come out of the cellars under their saloons. Good joke, isn't it?" And Snap laughed till a crack came in his neck and made him cough.

Lily was so surprised she sat down on a warm queen's cake that happened to be near, and watched Snap send down load after load of gingerbread to be eaten by children, who would have liked it much better if they had only known where it came from, as she did.

As she sat, the clatter of many spoons, the smell of many dinners, and the sound of many voices calling, "One vanilla, two strawberries, and a Charlotte Russe," "Three stews, cup coffee, dry toast," "Roast chicken and apple without," came up the next hole, which was marked "Copeland."

"Dear me! it seems as if I was there," said Lily, longing to hop down, but afraid of the bump at the other end.

"I'm done. Come along, I'll ride you back," called Snap, tossing the last cooky after the dumb-waiter as it went slowly out of sight with its spicy load.

"I wish you'd teach me to cook. It looks great fun, and mamma wants me to learn; only our cook hates to have me mess round, and is so cross that I don't like to try at home," said Lily, as she went trundling back.

"Better wait till you get to Bread-land, and learn to make that. It's a great art, and worth knowing. Don't waste your time on cake, though plain gingerbread isn't bad to have in the house. I'll teach you that in a jiffy, if the clock doesn't strike my hour too soon," answered Snap, helping her down.

"What hour?"

"Why, of my freedom. I never know when I've done my task till I'm called by the chimes and go to get my soul," said Snap, turning his currant eyes anxiously to the clock.

"I hope you *will* have time." And Lily fell to work with all her might, after Snap had put on her a paper apron and a cap like his.

It was not hard; for when she was going to make a mistake, a spark flew out of the fire and burnt her in time to remind her to look at the receipt, which was a sheet of gingerbread in a frame of pie-crust hung up before her, with the directions written while it was soft and baked in. The third sheet she made came out of the oven spicy, light, and brown; and Snap, giving it one poke, said, "That's all right. Now you know. Here's your reward."

He handed her a receipt-book made of thin sheets of sugar-gingerbread held together by a gelatine binding, with her name stamped on the back, and each leaf crimped with a cake-cutter in the most elegant manner.

Lily was charmed with it, but had no time to read all it contained; for just then the clock began to strike, and a chime of bells to ring, —

>"Gingerbread,
>Go to the head.
>Your task is done;
>A soul is won.
>Take it and go
>Where muffins grow,
>Where sweet loaves rise
>To the very skies,
>And biscuits fair
>Perfume the air.
>Away, away!
>Make no delay;
>In the sea of flour
>Plunge this hour.
>Safe in your breast
>Let the yeast-cake rest,
>Till you rise in joy,
>A white bread boy!"

"Ha, ha! I'm free! I'm free!" cried Snap, catching up the silver-covered square that seemed to fall from heaven; and running to a great white sea of flour, he went in head first, holding the yeast-cake clasped to his breast as if his life depended on it.

Lily watched breathlessly, while a curious working and bubbling went on, as if Snap was tumbling about down there like a small earthquake. The other cake-folk stood round the shore with her; for it was a great event, and all were glad that the dear fellow was promoted so soon. Suddenly a cry was heard, and up rose a beautiful white figure on the farther side of the sea. It moved its hand, as if saying "Goodby," and ran over the hills so fast they had only time to see how plump and fair he was, with a little knob on the top of his head like a crown.

"He's gone to the happy land, and we shall miss him; but we'll follow his example and soon find him again," said a gentle Sponge cake, with a sigh, as all went back to their work; while Lily hurried after Snap, eager to see the new country, which was the best of all.

A delicious odor of fresh bread blew up from the valley as she stood on the hill-top and looked down on the peaceful scene below. Fields of yellow grain waved in the breeze; hop-vines grew from tree to tree; and many windmills whirled their white sails as they ground the different grains into fresh, sweet meal, for the loaves of bread that built the houses like bricks and paved the streets, or in many shapes formed the people, furniture, and animals. A river of milk flowed through the peaceful land, and fountains of yeast rose and fell with a pleasant foam and fizz. The ground was a mixture of many meals, and the paths were golden Indian, which gave a very gay look to the scene. Buckwheat flowers bloomed on their rosy stems, and tall corn-stalks rustled their leaves in the warm air that came from the ovens hidden in the hillsides; for bread needs a slow fire, and an obliging volcano did the baking here.

"What a lovely place!" cried Lily, feeling the charm of the homelike landscape, in spite of the funny plump people moving about.

Two of these figures came running to meet her as she slowly walked down the yellow path from the hill. One was a golden boy, with a beaming face; the other a little girl in a shiny brown cloak, who looked as if she would taste very nice. They each put a warm hand into Lily's and the boy said, —

"We are glad to see you. Muffin told us you were coming."

"Thank you. Who is Muffin?" asked Lily, feeling as if she had seen both these little people before, and liked them.

"He was Ginger Snap once, but he's a Muffin now. We begin in that way, and work up to the perfect loaf by degrees. My name is Johnny Cake, and she's Sally Lunn. You know us; so come on and have a race."

Lily burst out laughing at the idea of playing with these old friends of hers; and all three ran away as fast as they could tear, down the hill, over a bridge, into the middle of the village, where they stopped, panting, and sat down on some very soft rolls to rest.

"What do you all do *here?*" asked Lily, when she got her breath again.

"We farm, we study, we bake, we brew, and are as merry as grigs all day long. It's school-time now, and we must go; will you come?" said Sally, jumping up as if she liked it.

"Our schools are not like yours; we only study two things, — grain and yeast. I think you'll like it. We have yeast to-day, and the experiments are very jolly," added Johnny, trotting off to a tall brown tower of rye and Indian bread, where the school was kept.

Lily never liked to go to school, but she was

ashamed to own it; so she went along with Sally, and was so amused with all she saw that she was glad she came. The brown loaf was hollow, and had no roof; and when she asked why they used a ruin, Sally told her to wait and see why they chose strong walls and plenty of room overhead. All round was a circle of very small biscuits like cushions, and on these the Bread-children sat. A square loaf in the middle was the teacher's desk, and on it lay an ear of wheat, with several bottles of yeast well corked up. The teacher was a pleasant, plump lady from Vienna, very wise, and so famous for her good bread that she was a Professor of Grainology.

When all were seated, she began with the wheat ear, and told them all about it in such an interesting way that Lily felt as if she had never known anything about the bread she ate before. The experiments with the yeast were quite exciting, — for Fraulein Pretzel showed them how it would work till it blew the cork out, and go fizzing up to the sky if it was kept too long; how it would turn sour or flat, and spoil the bread if care was not taken to use it just at the right moment; and how too much would cause the loaf to rise till there was no substance to it.

The children were very bright; for they were fed

on the best kinds of oatmeal and Graham bread, with very little white bread or hot cakes to spoil their young stomachs. Hearty, happy boys and girls they were, and their yeasty souls were very lively in them; for they danced and sung, and seemed as bright and gay as if acidity, heaviness, and mould were quite unknown.

Lily was very happy with them, and when school was done went home with Sally and ate the best bread and milk for dinner that she ever tasted. In the afternoon Johnny took her to the cornfield, and showed her how they kept the growing ears free from mildew and worms. Then she went to the bakehouse; and here she found her old friend Muffin hard at work making Parker House rolls, for he was such a good cook he was set to work at once on the lighter kinds of bread.

"Well, isn't this better than Candy-land or Saccharissa?" he asked, as he rolled and folded his bits of dough with a dab of butter tucked inside.

"Ever so much!" cried Lily. "I feel better already, and mean to learn all I can. Mamma will be so pleased if I can make good bread when I go home. She is rather old-fashioned, and likes me to be a nice housekeeper. I didn't think bread interesting then, but I do now; and Johnny's mother is going to teach me to make Indian cakes to-morrow."

"Glad to hear it. Learn all you can, and tell other people how to make healthy bodies and happy souls by eating good plain food. Not like this, though these rolls are better than cake. I have to work my way up to the perfect loaf, you know; and then, oh, then, I'm a happy thing."

"What happens then? Do you go on to some other wonderful place?" asked Lily, as Muffin paused with a smile on his face.

"Yes; I am eaten by some wise, good human being, and become a part of him or her. That is immortality and heaven; for I may nourish a poet and help him sing, or feed a good woman who makes the world better for being in it, or be crumbed into the golden porringer of a baby prince who is to rule a kingdom. Isn't that a noble way to live, and an end worth working for?" asked Muffin, in a tone that made Lily feel as if some sort of fine yeast had got into her, and was setting her brain to work with new thoughts.

"Yes, it is. I suppose all common things are made for that purpose, if we only knew it; and people should be glad to do anything to help the world along, even making good bread in a kitchen," answered Lily, in a sober way that showed that her little mind was already digesting the new food it had got.

She stayed in Bread-land a long time, and enjoyed and learned a great deal that she never forgot. But at last, when she had made the perfect loaf, she wanted to go home, that her mother might see and taste it.

"I've put a good deal of myself into it, and I'd love to think I had given her strength or pleasure by my work," she said, as she and Sally stood looking at the handsome loaf.

"You can go whenever you like; just take the bread in your hands and wish three times, and you'll be wherever you say. I'm sorry to have you go, but I don't wonder you want to see your mother. Don't forget what you have learned, and you will always be glad you came to us," said Sally, kissing her good-by.

"Where is Muffin? I can't go without seeing him, my dear old friend," answered Lily, looking round for him.

"He is here," said Sally, touching the loaf. "He was ready to go, and chose to pass into your bread rather than any other; for he said he loved you and would be glad to help feed so good a little girl."

"How kind of him! I must be careful to grow wise and excellent, else he will be disappointed and have died in vain," said Lily, touched by his devotion.

The Candy Country

Then, bidding them all farewell, she hugged her loaf close, wished three times to be in her own home, and like a flash she was there.

Whether her friends believed the wonderful tale of her adventures I cannot tell; but I know that she was a nice little housekeeper from that day, and made such good bread that other girls came to learn of her. She also grew from a sickly, fretful child into a fine, strong woman, because she ate very little cake and candy, except at Christmas time, when the oldest and the wisest love to make a short visit to Candy-land.

SOPHIE'S SECRET

I

A PARTY of young girls, in their gay bathing-dresses, were sitting on the beach waiting for the tide to rise a little higher before they enjoyed the daily frolic which they called "mermaiding."

"I wish we could have a clam-bake; but we haven't any clams, and don't know how to cook them if we had. It's such a pity all the boys have gone off on that stupid fishing excursion," said one girl, in a yellow-and-black striped suit which made her look like a wasp.

"What is a clam-bake? I do not know that kind of fête," asked a pretty brown-eyed girl, with an accent that betrayed the foreigner.

The girls laughed at such sad ignorance, and Sophie colored, wishing she had not spoken.

"Poor thing! she has never tasted a clam. What *should* we do if we went to Switzerland?" said the wasp, who loved to tease.

"We should give you the best we had, and not laugh at your ignorance, if you did not know all our dishes. In *my* country, we have politeness, though not the clam-bake," answered Sophie, with a flash of the brown eyes which warned naughty Di to desist.

"We might row to the light-house, and have a picnic supper. Our mammas will let us do that alone," suggested Dora from the roof of the bath-house, where she perched like a flamingo.

"That's a good idea," cried Fanny, a slender brown girl who sat dabbling her feet in the water, with her hair streaming in the wind. "Sophie should see that, and get some of the shells she likes so much."

"You are kind to think of me. I shall be glad to have a necklace of the pretty things, as a souvenir of this so charming place and my good friend," answered Sophie, with a grateful look at Fanny, whose many attentions had won the stranger's heart.

"Those boys haven't left us a single boat, so we must dive off the rocks, and that isn't half so nice," said Di, to change the subject, being ashamed of her rudeness.

"A boat is just coming round the Point; perhaps we can hire that, and have some fun," cried Dora, from her perch. "There is only a girl in it; I'll hail her when she is near enough."

Sophie looked about her to see where the *hail*

was coming from; but the sky was clear, and she waited to see what new meaning this word might have, not daring to ask for fear of another laugh.

While the girls watched the boat float around the farther horn of the crescent-shaped beach, we shall have time to say a few words about our little heroine.

She was a sixteen-year-old Swiss girl, on a visit to some American friends, and had come to the seaside for a month with one of them who was an invalid. This left Sophie to the tender mercies of the young people; and they gladly welcomed the pretty creature, with her fine manners, foreign ways, and many accomplishments. But she had a quick temper, a funny little accent, and dressed so very plainly that the girls could not resist criticising and teasing her in a way that seemed very ill-bred and unkind to the new-comer.

Their free and easy ways astonished her, their curious language bewildered her; and their ignorance of many things she had been taught made her wonder at the American education she had heard so much praised. All had studied French and German; yet few read or spoke either tongue correctly, or understood her easily when she tried to talk to them. Their music did not amount to much, and in the

Sophie's Secret 119

games they played, their want of useful information amazed Sophie. One did not know the signs of the zodiac; another could only say of cotton that "it was stuff that grew down South;" and a third was not sure whether a frog was an animal or a reptile, while the handwriting and spelling displayed on these occasions left much to be desired. Yet all were fifteen or sixteen, and would soon leave school "finished," as they expressed it, but not *furnished*, as they should have been, with a solid, sensible education. Dress was an all-absorbing topic, sweetmeats their delight; and in confidential moments sweethearts were discussed with great freedom. Fathers were conveniences, mothers comforters, brothers plagues, and sisters ornaments or playthings according to their ages. They were not hard-hearted girls, only frivolous, idle, and fond of fun; and poor little Sophie amused them immensely till they learned to admire, love, and respect her.

Coming straight from Paris, they expected to find that her trunks contained the latest fashions for demoiselles, and begged to see her dresses with girlish interest. But when Sophie obligingly showed a few simple, but pretty and appropriate gowns and hats, they exclaimed with one voice, —

"Why, you dress like a little girl! Don't you have

ruffles and lace on your dresses; and silks and high-heeled boots and long gloves and bustles and corsets, and things like ours?"

"I *am* a little girl," laughed Sophie, hardly understanding their dismay. "What should I do with fine toilets at school? My sisters go to balls in silk and lace; but I — not yet."

"How queer! Is your father poor?" asked Di, with Yankee bluntness.

"We have enough," answered Sophie, slightly knitting her dark brows.

"How many servants do you keep?"

"But five, now that the little ones are grown up."

"Have you a piano?" continued undaunted Di, while the others affected to be looking at the books and pictures strewn about by the hasty unpacking.

"We have two pianos, four violins, three flutes, and an organ. We love music, and all play, from papa to little Franz."

"My gracious, how swell! You must live in a big house to hold all that and eight brothers and sisters."

"We are not peasants; we do not live in a hut. *Voilà*, this is my home." And Sophie laid before them a fine photograph of a large and elegant house on lovely Lake Geneva.

It was droll to see the change in the faces of the

girls as they looked, admired, and slyly nudged one another, enjoying saucy Di's astonishment, for she had stoutly insisted that the Swiss girl was a poor relation.

Sophie meanwhile was folding up her plain piqué and muslin frocks, with a glimmer of mirthful satisfaction in her eyes, and a tender pride in the work of loving hands now far away.

Kind Fanny saw a little quiver of the lips as she smoothed the blue corn-flowers in the best hat, and put her arm around Sophie, whispering, —

"Never mind, dear, they don't mean to be rude; it's only our Yankee way of asking questions. I like *all* your things, and that hat is perfectly lovely."

"Indeed, yes! Dear mamma arranged it for me. I was thinking of her and longing for my morning kiss."

"Do you do that every day?" asked Fanny, forgetting herself in her sympathetic interest.

"Surely, yes. Papa and mamma sit always on the sofa, and we all have the hand-shake and the embrace each day before our morning coffee. I do not see that here," answered Sophie, who sorely missed the affectionate respect foreign children give their parents.

"Haven't time," said Fanny, smiling too, at the

idea of American parents sitting still for five minutes in the busiest part of the busy day to kiss their sons and daughters.

"It is what you call old-fashioned, but a sweet fashion to me; and since I have not the dear warm cheeks to kiss, I embrace my pictures often. See, I have them all." And Sophie unfolded a Russia-leather case, displaying with pride a long row of handsome brothers and sisters with the parents in the midst.

More exclamations from the girls, and increased interest in "Wilhelmina Tell," as they christened the loyal Swiss maiden, who was now accepted as a companion, and soon became a favorite with old and young.

They could not resist teasing her, however, — her mistakes were so amusing, her little flashes of temper so dramatic, and her tongue so quick to give a sharp or witty answer when the new language did not perplex her. But Fanny always took her part, and helped her in many ways. Now they sat together on the rock, a pretty pair of mermaids with wind-tossed hair, wave-washed feet, and eyes fixed on the approaching boat.

The girl who sat in it was a great contrast to the gay creatures grouped so picturesquely on the shore, for the old straw hat shaded a very anxious face, the brown calico gown covered a heart full of hopes and fears, and the boat that drifted so slowly with the incoming tide carried Tilly Reed like a young Columbus toward the new world she longed for, believed in, and was resolved to discover.

It was a weather-beaten little boat, yet very pretty; for a pile of nets lay at one end, a creel of red lobsters at the other, and all between stood baskets of berries and water-lilies, purple marsh rosemary and orange butterfly-weed, shells and great smooth stones such as artists like to paint little sea-views on. A tame gull perched on the prow; and the morning sunshine glittered from the blue water to the bluer sky.

"Oh, how pretty! Come on, please, and sell us some lilies," cried Dora, and roused Tilly from her waking dream.

Pushing back her hat, she saw the girls beckoning, felt that the critical moment had come, and catching up her oars, rowed bravely on, though her cheeks reddened and her heart beat, for this venture was her last hope, and on its success depended the desire of her life. As the boat approached, the watchers forgot its cargo to look with surprise and pleasure at its rower, for she was not the rough country lass they expected to see, but a really splendid girl of fifteen, tall, broad-shouldered, bright-eyed, and blooming, with a certain shy dignity of her own and a very sweet smile, as she nodded and pulled in with strong, steady strokes. Before they could offer help, she had risen, planted an oar in the water, and leaping to the shore, pulled her boat high up on the beach, offering her wares with wistful eyes and a very expressive wave of both brown hands.

"Everything is for sale, if you'll buy," said she.

Charmed with the novelty of this little adventure, the girls, after scampering to the bathing-houses for purses and portemonnaies, crowded around the boat like butterflies about a thistle, all eager to buy, and to discover who this bonny fisher-maiden might be.

"Oh, see these beauties!" "A dozen lilies for me!" "All the yellow flowers for me, they'll be so becoming at the dance to-night!" "Ow! that lob bites awfully!" "Where do you come from?" "Why have we never seen you before?"

These were some of the exclamations and questions showered upon Tilly, as she filled little birch-bark panniers with berries, dealt out flowers, or dispensed handfuls of shells. Her eyes shone, her cheeks glowed, and her heart danced in her bosom; for this was a better beginning than she had dared to hope for, and as the dimes tinkled into the tin pail she used for her till, it was the sweetest music she had ever heard. This hearty welcome banished her shyness; and in these eager, girlish customers she found it easy to confide.

"I'm from the light-house. You have never seen me because I never came before, except with fish for the hotel. But I mean to come every day, if folks will buy my things, for I want to make some money, and this is the only way in which I can do it."

Sophie glanced at the old hat and worn shoes of the speaker, and dropping a bright half-dollar into the pail, said in her pretty way:

"For me all these lovely shells. I will make necklaces of them for my people at home as souvenirs of this charming place. If you will bring me more, I shall be much grateful to you."

"Oh, thank you! I'll bring heaps; I know where to find beauties in places where other folks can't go. Please take these; you paid too much for the shells;" and quick to feel the kindness of the stranger, Tilly put into her hands a little bark canoe heaped with red raspberries.

Not to be outdone by the foreigner, the other

girls emptied their purses and Tilly's boat also of all but the lobsters, which were ordered for the hotel.

"Is that jolly bird for sale?" asked Di, as the last berry vanished, pointing to the gull who was swimming near them while the chatter went on.

"If you can catch him," laughed Tilly, whose spirits were now the gayest of the party.

The girls dashed into the water, and with shrieks of merriment swam away to capture the gull, who paddled off as if he enjoyed the fun as much as they.

Leaving them to splash vainly to and fro, Tilly swung the creel to her shoulder and went off to leave her lobsters, longing to dance and sing to the music of the silver clinking in her pocket.

When she came back, the bird was far out of reach and the girls diving from her boat, which they had launched without leave. Too happy to care what happened now, Tilly threw herself down on the warm sand to plan a new and still finer cargo for next day.

Sophie came and sat beside her while she dried her curly hair, and in five minutes her sympathetic face and sweet ways had won Tilly to tell all her hopes and cares and dreams.

"I want schooling, and I mean to have it. I've got no folks of my own; and uncle has married again, so he doesn't need me now. If I only had a little money, I could go to school somewhere, and take care of myself. Last summer I worked at the hotel, but I didn't make much, and had to have good clothes, and that took my wages pretty much. Sewing is slow work, and baby-tending leaves me no time to study; so I've kept on at home picking berries and doing what I could to pick up enough to buy books. Aunt thinks I'm a fool; but uncle, he says, 'Go ahead, girl, and see what you can do.' And I mean to show him!"

Tilly's brown hand came down on the sand with a resolute thump; and her clear young eyes looked bravely out across the wide sea, as if far away in the blue distance she saw her hope happily fulfilled.

Sophie's eyes shone approval, for she understood this love of independence, and had come to America because she longed for new scenes and greater freedom than her native land could give her. Education is a large word, and both girls felt that desire for self-improvement that comes to all energetic natures. Sophie had laid a good foundation, but still desired more; while Tilly was just climbing up the first steep slope which rises to the heights few attain, yet all may strive for.

"That is beautiful! You will do it! I am glad to

help you if I may. See, I have many books; will you take some of them? Come to my room to-morrow and take what will best please you. We will say nothing of it, and it will make me a truly great pleasure."

As Sophie spoke, her little white hand touched the strong, sunburned one that turned to meet and grasp hers with grateful warmth, while Tilly's face betrayed the hunger that possessed her, for it looked as a starving girl's would look when offered a generous meal.

"I *will* come. Thank you so much! I don't know anything, but just blunder along and do the best I can. I got so discouraged I was real desperate, and thought I'd have one try, and see if I couldn't earn enough to get books to study this winter. Folks buy berries at the cottages; so I just added flowers and shells, and I'm going to bring my boxes of butterflies, birds' eggs, and seaweeds. I've got lots of such things; and people seem to like spending money down here. I often wish I had a little of what they throw away."

Tilly paused with a sigh, then laughed as an impatient movement caused a silver clink; and slapping her pocket, she added gayly, —

"I won't blame 'em if they'll only throw their money in here."

Sophie's hand went involuntarily toward her own pocket, where lay a plump purse, for papa was generous, and simple Sophie had few wants. But something in the intelligent face opposite made her hesitate to offer as a gift what she felt sure Tilly would refuse, preferring to earn her education if she could.

"Come often, then, and let me exchange these stupid bills for the lovely things you bring. We will come this afternoon to see you if we may, and I shall like the butterflies. I try to catch them; but people tell me I am too old to run, so I have not many."

Proposed in this way, Tilly fell into the little trap, and presently rowed away with all her might to set her possessions in order, and put her precious earnings in a safe place. The mermaids clung about the boat as long as they dared, making a pretty tableau for the artists on the rocks, then swam to shore, more than ever eager for the picnic on Light-house Island.

They went, and had a merry time; while Tilly did the honors and showed them a room full of treasures gathered from earth, air, and water, for she led a lonely life, and found friends among the fishes, made playmates of the birds, and studied rocks and flowers, clouds and waves, when books were wanting.

The girls bought gulls' wings for their hats, queer and lovely shells, eggs and insects, sea-weeds and carved wood, and for their small brothers, birch baskets and toy ships, made by Uncle Hiram, who had been a sailor.

When Tilly had sold nearly everything she possessed (for Fanny and Sophie bought whatever the others declined), she made a fire of drift-wood on the rocks, cooked fish for supper, and kept them till moonrise, telling sea stories or singing old songs, as if she could not do enough for these good fairies who had come to her when life looked hardest and the future very dark. Then she rowed them home, and promising to bring loads of fruit and flowers every day, went back along a shining road, to find a great bundle of books in her dismantled room, and to fall asleep with wet eyelashes and a happy heart.

II

For a month Tilly went daily to the Point with a cargo of pretty merchandise, for her patrons increased; and soon the ladies engaged her berries, the boys ordered boats enough to supply a navy, the children clamored for shells, and the girls depended on her for bouquets and garlands for the dances that ended every summer day. Uncle Hiram's fish was in demand when such a comely saleswoman offered it; so he let Tilly have her way, glad to see the old tobacco-pouch in which she kept her cash fill fast with well-earned money.

She really began to feel that her dream was coming true, and she would be able to go to the town and study in some great school, eking out her little fund with light work. The other girls soon lost their interest in her, but Sophie never did; and many a book went to the island in the empty baskets, many a helpful word was said over the lilies or wild honeysuckle Sophie loved to wear, and many a lesson was given in the bare room in the light-house tower which no one knew about but the gulls and the sea-winds sweeping by the little window where the two heads leaned together over one page.

"You will do it, Tilly, I am very sure. Such a will and such a memory will make a way for you; and one day I shall see you teaching as you wish. Keep the brave heart, and all will be well with you," said Sophie, when the grand breaking-up came in September, and the girls were parting down behind the deserted bath-houses.

"Oh, Miss Sophie, what should I have done without you? Don't think I haven't seen and known all the kind things you have said and done for me. I'll never forget 'em; and I do hope I'll be able to thank you some day," cried grateful Tilly, with tears in her clear eyes that seldom wept over her own troubles.

"I am thanked if you do well. Adieu; write to me, and remember always that I am your friend."

Then they kissed with girlish warmth, and Tilly rowed away to the lonely island; while Sophie lingered on the shore, her handkerchief fluttering in the wind, till the boat vanished and the waves had washed away their footprints on the sand.

III

December snow was falling fast, and the wintry wind whistled through the streets; but it was warm and cozy in the luxurious parlor where Di and Do were sitting making Christmas presents, and planning what they would wear at the party Fanny was to give on Christmas Eve.

"If I can get mamma to buy me a new dress, I shall have something yellow. It is always becoming to brunettes, and I'm so tired of red," said Di, giving a last touch to the lace that trimmed a blue satin *sachet* for Fanny.

"That will be lovely. I shall have pink, with roses of the same color. Under muslin it is perfectly sweet." And Dora eyed the sunflower she was embroidering as if she already saw the new toilet before her.

"Fan always wears blue, so we shall make a nice contrast. She is coming over to show me about finishing off my banner-screen; and I asked Sophie to come with her. I want to know what *she* is going to wear," said Di, taking a little sniff at the violet-scented bag.

"That old white cashmere. Just think! I asked her why she didn't get a new one, and she laughed and said she couldn't afford it. Fan told me Sophie's father sent her a hundred dollars not long ago, yet she hasn't got a thing that we know of. I do think she's mean."

"She bought a great bundle of books. I was there when the parcel came, and I peeped while she was out of the room, because she put it away in a great hurry. I'm afraid she *is* mean, for she never buys a bit of candy, and she wears shabby boots and gloves, and she has made over her old hat instead of having that lovely one with the pheasant's breast in it."

"She's very queer; but I can't help liking her, she's so pretty and bright and obliging. I'd give anything if I could speak three languages and play as she does."

"So would I. It seems so elegant to be able to talk to foreigners. Papa had some Frenchmen to dinner the other day, and they were so pleased to find they needn't speak English to Sophie. I couldn't get on at all; and I was so mortified when papa said all the money he had spent on my languages was thrown away."

"I wouldn't mind. It's so much easier to learn those things abroad, she would be a goose if she didn't speak French better than we do. There's Fan! she looks as if something had happened. I hope no one is ill and the party spoiled."

As Dora spoke, both girls looked out to see Fanny shaking the snow from her seal-skin sack on the doorstep; then Do hastened to meet her, while Di hid the *sachet*, and was hard at work on an old-gold sofa cushion when the new-comer entered.

"What's the matter? Where's Sophie?" exclaimed the girls together, as Fan threw off her wraps and sat down with a tragic sigh.

"She will be along in a few minutes. I'm disappointed in her! I wouldn't have believed it if I hadn't seen them. Promise not to breathe a word to a living soul, and I'll tell you something dreadful," began Fanny, in a tone that caused her friends to drop their work and draw their chairs nearer, as they solemnly vowed eternal silence.

"I've seen Sophie's Christmas presents, — all but mine; and they are just nothing at all! She hasn't bought a thing, not even ribbons, lace, or silk, to make up prettily as we do. Only a painted shell for one, an acorn emery for another, her ivory fan with a new tassel for a third, and I suspect one of those nice handkerchiefs embroidered by the nuns for me, or her silver filigree necklace. I saw the box in the drawer with the other things. She's knit woollen cuffs and tippets for the children, and got some eight-cent calico gowns for the servants. I don't know how people do things in Switzerland, but I do know that if *I* had a hundred dollars in my pocket, I would be more generous than that!"

As Fanny paused, out of breath, Di and Do groaned in sympathy, for this was indeed a sad state of things; because the girls had a code that Christmas being the season for gifts, extravagance would be forgiven then as at no other time.

"I have a lovely smelling-bottle for her; but I've a great mind not to give it now," cried Di, feeling defrauded of the bracelet she had plainly hinted she would like.

"I shall heap coals of fire on her head by giving her *that;*" and Dora displayed a very useless but very pretty apron of muslin, lace, and carnation ribbon.

"It isn't the worth of the things. I don't care for that so much as I do for being disappointed in her; and I have been lately in more ways than one," said Fanny, listlessly taking up the screen she was to finish. "She used to tell me everything, and now she doesn't. I'm sure she has some sort of a secret; and I do think *I* ought to know it. I found her smiling over a letter one day; and she whisked it into her pocket and never said a word about it. I always stood by her, and I do feel hurt."

"I should think you might! It's real naughty of her, and I shall tell her so! Perhaps she'll confide in you then, and you can just give *me* a hint; I always liked Sophie, and never thought of not giving *my* present," said Dora, persuasively, for both girls were now dying with curiosity to know the secret.

"I'll have it out of her, without any dodging or bribing. I'm not afraid of any one, and I shall ask her straight out, no matter how much she scowls at me," said dauntless Di, with a threatening nod.

"There she is! Let us see you do it now!" cried

Fanny, as the bell rang, and a clear voice was heard a moment later asking if Mademoiselle was in.

"You shall!" and Di looked ready for any audacity.

"I'll wager a box of candy that you don't find out a thing," whispered Do.

"Done!" answered Di, and then turned to meet Sophie, who came in looking as fresh as an Alpine rose with the wintry wind.

"You dear thing! we were just talking of you. Sit here and get warm, and let us show you our gifts. We are almost done, but it seems as if it got to be a harder job each Christmas. Don't you find it so?"

"But no; I think it the most charming work of all the year," answered Sophie, greeting her friend, and putting her well-worn boots toward the fire to dry.

"Perhaps you don't make as much of Christmas as we do, or give such expensive presents. That would make a great difference, you know," said Di, as she lifted a cloth from the table where her own generous store of gifts was set forth.

"I had a piano last year, a set of jewels, and many pretty trifles from all at home. Here is one;" and pulling the fine gold chain hidden under her frills,

Sophie showed a locket set thick with pearls, containing a picture of her mother.

"It must be so nice to be rich, and able to make such fine presents. I've got something for you; but I shall be ashamed of it after I see your gift to me, I'm afraid."

Fan and Dora were working as if their bread depended on it, while Di, with a naughty twinkle in her eye, affected to be rearranging her pretty table as she talked.

"Do not fear that; my gifts this year are very simple ones. I did not know your custom, and now it is too late. My comfort is that you need nothing, and having so much, you will not care for my — what you call — coming short."

Was it the fire that made Sophie's face look so hot, and a cold that gave a husky sort of tone to her usually clear voice? A curious expression came into her face as her eyes roved from the table to the gay trifles in her friend's hands; and she opened her lips as if to add something impulsively. But nothing came, and for a moment she looked straight out at the storm as if she had forgotten where she was.

"'Shortcoming' is the proper way to speak it. But never mind that, and tell me why you say 'too late'?" asked Di, bent on winning her wager.

"Christmas comes in three days, and I have no time," began Sophie.

"But with money one can buy plenty of lovely things in one day," said Di.

"No, it is better to put a little love and hard work into what we give to friends. I have done that with my trifles, and another year I shall be more ready."

There was an uncomfortable pause, for Sophie did not speak with her usual frankness, but looked both proud and ashamed, and seemed anxious to change the subject, as she began to admire Dora's work, which had made very little progress during the last fifteen minutes.

Fanny glanced at Di with a smile that made the other toss her head and return to the charge with renewed vigor.

"Sophie, will you do me a favor?"

"With much pleasure."

"Do has promised me a whole box of French bonbons, and if you will answer three questions, you shall have it."

"*Allons*," said Sophie, smiling.

"Haven't you a secret?" asked Di, gravely.

"Yes."

"Will you tell us?"

"No."

Di paused before she asked her last question, and Fan and Dora waited breathlessly, while Sophie knit her brows and looked uneasy.

"Why not?"

"Because I do not wish to tell it."

"Will you tell if we guess?"

"Try."

"You are engaged."

At this absurd suggestion Sophie laughed gayly, and shook her curly head.

"Do you think we are betrothed at sixteen in my country?"

"I *know* that is an engagement ring, — you made such a time about it when you lost it in the water, and cried for joy when Tilly dived and found it."

"Ah, yes, I was truly glad. Dear Tilly, never do I forget that kindness!" and Sophie kissed the little pearl ring in her impulsive way, while her eyes sparkled and the frown vanished.

"I *know* a sweetheart gave it," insisted Di, sure now she had found a clew to the secret.

"He did," and Sophie hung her head in a sentimental way that made the three girls crowd nearer with faces full of interest.

"Do tell us all about it, dear. It's *so* interesting to hear love-stories. What is his name?" cried Dora.

"Hermann," simpered Sophie, drooping still more, while her lips trembled with suppressed emotion of some sort.

"How lovely!" sighed Fanny, who was very romantic.

"Tell on, do! Is he handsome?"

"To me the finest man in all the world," confessed Sophie, as she hid her face.

"And you love him?"

"I adore him!" and Sophie clasped her hands so dramatically that the girls were a little startled, yet charmed at this discovery.

"Have you his picture?" asked Di, feeling that she had won her wager now.

"Yes," and pulling out the locket again, Sophie showed in the other side the face of a fine old gentleman who looked very like herself.

"It's your father!" exclaimed Fanny, rolling her blue eyes excitedly. "You are a humbug!" cried Dora. "Then you fibbed about the ring," said Di, crossly.

"Never! It is mamma's betrothal ring; but her finger grew too plump, and when I left home, she gave the ring to me as a charm to keep me safe. Ah, ha! I have my little joke as well as you, and the laugh is for me this time." And falling back among the sofa cushions, Sophie enjoyed it as only a gay girl could. Do and Fanny joined her; but Di was much disgusted, and vowed she *would* discover the secret and keep all the bonbons to herself.

"You are most welcome; but I will not tell until I like, and then to Fanny first. She will not have ridicule for what I do, but say it is well, and be glad with me. Come now and work. I will plait these ribbons, or paint a wild rose on this pretty fan. It is too plain now. Will you that I do it, dear Di?"

The kind tone and the prospect of such an ornament to her gift appeased Di somewhat; but the mirthful malice in Sophie's eyes made the other more than ever determined to be even with her by and by.

Christmas Eve came, and found Di still in the dark, which fact nettled her sadly, for Sophie tormented her and amused the other girls by pretended confidences and dark hints at the mystery which might never, never be disclosed.

Fan had determined to have an unusually jolly party; so she invited only her chosen friends, and opened the festivities with a Christmas tree, as the prettiest way of exchanging gifts and providing jokes for the evening in the shape of delusive bottles, animals full of candy, and every sort of musical instrument to be used in an impromptu concert afterward. The presents to one another were done up in secure parcels, so that they might burst upon the public eye in all their freshness. Di was very curious to know what Fan was going to give her, — for Fanny was a generous creature and loved to give. Di was a little jealous of her love for Sophie, and couldn't rest till she discovered which was to get the finer gift.

So she went early and slipped into the room where the tree stood, to peep and pick a bit, as well as to hang up a few trifles of her own. She guessed several things by feeling the parcels; but one excited her curiosity intensely, and she could not resist turning it about and pulling up one corner of the lid. It was a flat box, prettily ornamented with sea-weeds like red lace, and tied with scarlet ribbons. A tantalizing glimpse of jeweller's cotton, gold clasps, and something rose-colored conquered Di's last scruples; and she was just about to untie the ribbons when she heard Fanny's voice, and had only time to replace the box, pick up a paper that had fallen out of it, and fly up the back stairs to the dressing-room, where she found Sophie and Dora surveying each other as girls always do before they go down.

"You look like a daisy," cried Di, admiring Dora with great interest, because she felt ashamed of her prying, and the stolen note in her pocket.

"And you like a dandelion," returned Do, falling back a step to get a good view of Di's gold-colored dress and black velvet bows.

"Sophie is a lily of the valley, all in green and white," added Fanny, coming in with her own blue skirts waving in the breeze.

"It does me very well. Little girls do not need grand toilets, and I am fine enough for a 'peasant,'" laughed Sophie, as she settled the fresh ribbons on her simple white cashmere and the holly wreath in her brown hair, but secretly longing for the fine dress she might have had.

"Why didn't you wear your silver necklace? It would be lovely on your pretty neck," said Di, longing to know if she had given the trinket away.

But Sophie was not to be caught, and said with a contented smile, "I do not care for ornaments unless some one I love gives me them. I had red roses for my *bouquet de corsage;* but the poor Madame Page was so *triste,* I left them on her table to remember her of me. It seemed so heartless to go and dance while she had only pain; but she wished it."

"Dear little Sophie, how good you are!" and

Sophie's Secret 145

warm-hearted Fan kissed the blooming face that needed no roses to make it sweet and gay.

Half an hour later, twenty girls and boys were dancing round the brilliant tree. Then its boughs were stripped. Every one seemed contented; even Sophie's little gifts gave pleasure, because with each went a merry or affectionate verse, which made great fun on being read aloud. She was quite loaded with pretty things, and had no words to express her gratitude and pleasure.

"Ah, you are all so good to me! and I have nothing beautiful for you. I receive much and give little, but I cannot help it! Wait a little and I will redeem myself," she said to Fanny, with eyes full of tears, and a lap heaped with gay and useful things.

"Never mind that now; but look at this, for here's still another offering of friendship, and a very charming one, to judge by the outside," answered Fan, bringing the white box with the sea-weed ornaments.

Sophie opened it, and cries of admiration followed, for lying on the soft cotton was a lovely set of coral. Rosy pink branches, highly polished and fastened with gold clasps, formed necklace, bracelets, and a spray for the bosom. No note or card appeared, and the girls crowded round to admire and wonder who could have sent so valuable a gift.

"Can't you guess, Sophie?" cried Dora, longing to own the pretty things.

"I should believe I knew, but it is too costly. How came the parcel, Fan? I think you must know all," and Sophie turned the box about, searching vainly for a name.

"An expressman left it, and Jane took off the wet paper and put it on my table with the other things. Here's the wrapper; do you know that writing?" and Fan offered the brown paper which she had kept.

"No; and the label is all mud, so I cannot see the place. Ah, well, I shall discover some day, but I should like to thank this generous friend at once. See now, how fine I am! I do myself the honor to wear them at once."

Smiling with girlish delight at her pretty ornaments, Sophie clasped the bracelets on her round arms, the necklace about her white throat, and set the rosy spray in the lace on her bosom. Then she took a little dance down the room and found herself before Di, who was looking at her with an expression of naughty satisfaction on her face.

"Don't you wish you knew who sent them?"

"Indeed, yes;" and Sophie paused abruptly.

"Well, *I* know, and *I* won't tell till I like. It's my turn to have a secret; and I mean to keep it."

"But it is not right," began Sophie, with indignation.

"Tell me yours, and I'll tell mine," said Di, teasingly.

"I will not! You have no right to touch my gifts, and I am sure you have done it, else how know you who sends this fine *cadeau?*" cried Sophie, with the flash Di liked to see.

Here Fanny interposed, "If you have any note or card belonging to Sophie, give it up at once. She shall not be tormented. Out with it, Di. I see your hand in your pocket, and I'm sure you have been in mischief."

"Take your old letter, then. I know what's in it; and if I can't keep my secret for fun, Sophie shall not have hers. That Tilly sent the coral, and Sophie spent her hundred dollars in books and clothes for that queer girl, who'd better stay among her lobsters than try to be a lady," cried Di, bent on telling all she knew, while Sophie was reading her letter eagerly.

"Is it true?" asked Dora, for the four girls were in a corner together, and the rest of the company busy pulling crackers.

"Just like her! I thought it was that; but she wouldn't tell. Tell us now, Sophie, for *I* think it was truly sweet and beautiful to help that poor girl, and let us say hard things of you," cried Fanny, as her friend looked up with a face and a heart too full of happiness to help overflowing into words.

"Yes; I will tell you now. It was foolish, perhaps; but I did not want to be praised, and I loved to help that good Tilly. You know she worked all summer and made a little sum. So glad, so proud she was, and planned to study that she might go to school this winter. Well, in October the uncle fell very ill, and Tilly gave all her money for the doctors. The uncle had been kind to her, she did not forget; she was glad to help, and told no one but me. Then I said, 'What better can I do with my father's gift than give it to the dear creature, and let her lose no time?' I do it; she will not at first, but I write and say, 'It must be,' and she submits. She is made neat with some little dresses, and she goes at last, to be so happy and do so well that I am proud of her. Is not that better than fine toilets and rich gifts to those who need nothing? Truly, yes! yet I confess it cost me pain to give up my plans for Christmas, and to seem selfish or ungrateful. Forgive me that."

"Yes, indeed, you dear generous thing!" cried Fan and Dora, touched by the truth.

"But how came Tilly to send you such a splendid present?" asked Di. "Shouldn't think you'd like her to spend your money in such things."

"She did not. A sea-captain, a friend of the uncle, gave her these lovely ornaments, and she sends them to me with a letter that is more precious than all the coral in the sea. I cannot read it; but of all my gifts *this* is the dearest and the best!"

Sophie had spoken eagerly, and her face, her voice, her gestures, made the little story eloquent; but with the last words she clasped the letter to her bosom as if it well repaid her for all the sacrifices she had made. They might seem small to others, but she was sensitive and proud, anxious to be loved in the strange country, and fond of giving, so it cost her many tears to seem mean and thoughtless, to go poorly dressed, and be thought hardly of by those she wished to please. She did not like to tell of her own generosity, because it seemed like boasting; and she was not sure that it had been wise to give so much. Therefore, she waited to see if Tilly was worthy of the trust reposed in her; and she now found a balm for many wounds in the loving letter that came with the beautiful and unexpected gift.

Di listened with hot cheeks, and when Sophie paused, she whispered regretfully, —

"Forgive me, I was wrong! I'll keep your gift all my life to remember you by, for you *are* the best and dearest girl I know."

Then with a hasty kiss she ran away, carrying with great care the white shell on which Sophie had painted a dainty little picture of the mermaids waiting for the pretty boat that brought good fortune to poor Tilly, and this lesson to those who were hereafter her faithful friends.

TRUDEL'S SIEGE

"GRANDMOTHER, what is this curious picture about?" said little Gertrude, or "Trudel," as they called her, looking up from the red book that lay on her knee, one Sunday morning, when she and the grandmother sat sadly together in the neat kitchen; for the father was very ill, and the poor mother seldom left him.

The old woman put on her round spectacles, which made her look as wise as an owl, and turned to answer the child, who had been as quiet as a mouse for a long time, looking at the strange pictures in the ancient book.

"Ah, my dear, that tells about a very famous and glorious thing that happened long ago at the siege of Leyden. You can read it for yourself some day."

"Please tell me now. Why are the houses half under water, and ships sailing among them, and people leaning over the walls of the city? And why is that boy waving his hands on the tower, where the men are running away in a great smoke?' asked Trudel, too curious to wait till she could read the long hard words on the yellow pages.

"Well, dear, this is the story: and you shall hear

how brave men and women, and children too, were in those days. The cruel Spaniards came and besieged the city for many months; but the faithful people would not give up, though nearly starved to death. When all the bread and meat were gone and the gardens empty, they ate grass and herbs and horses, and even dogs and cats, trying to hold out till help came to them."

"Did little girls really eat their pussies? Oh, I'd die before I would kill my dear Jan," cried Trudel, hugging the pretty kitten that purred in her lap.

"Yes, the children ate their pets. And so would you if it would save your father or mother from starving. *We* know what hunger is; but we won't eat Jan yet."

The old woman sighed as she glanced from the empty table to the hearth where no fire burned.

"*Did* help come in the ships?" asked the child, bending her face over the book to hide the tears that filled her eyes, for she was very hungry, and had had only a crust for breakfast.

"Our good Prince of Orange was trying to help them; but the Spaniards were all around the city and he had not men enough to fight them by land, so he sent carrier-doves with letters to tell the people that he was going to cut through the great dikes that kept the sea out, and let the water flow over the country so as to drive the enemy from his camp, for the city stood upon high ground, and would be safe. Then the ships, with food, could sail over the drowned land and save the brave people."

"Oh, I'm glad! I'm glad! These are the bad Spaniards running away, and these are poor people stretching out their hands for the bread. But what is the boy doing, in the funny tower where the wall has tumbled down?" cried Trudel, much excited.

"The smoke of burning houses rose between the city and the port so the people could not see that the Spaniards had run away; and they were afraid the ships could not get safely by. But a boy who was scrambling about as boys always are wherever there is danger, fire, and fighting, saw the enemy go, and ran to the deserted tower to shout and beckon to the ships to come on at once, — for the wind had changed and soon the tide would flow back and leave them stranded."

"Nice boy! I wish I had been there to see him and help the poor people," said Trudel, patting the funny little figure sticking out of the pepper-pot tower like a jack-in-the-box.

"If children keep their wits about them and are brave, they can always help in some way, my dear.

We don't have such dreadful wars now; but the dear God knows we have troubles enough, and need all our courage and faith to be patient in times like these;" and the grandmother folded her thin hands with another sigh, as she thought of her poor son dying for want of a few comforts, after working long and faithfully for a hard master who never came to offer any help, though a very rich man.

"Did they eat the carrier-doves?" asked Trudel, still intent on the story.

"No, child; they fed and cared for them while they lived, and when they died, stuffed and set them up in the Staat Haus, so grateful were the brave burghers for the good news the dear birds brought."

"That is the best part of all. I like that story very much!" And Trudel turned the pages to find another, little dreaming what a carrier-dove she herself was soon to become.

Poor Hans Dort and his family were nearly as distressed as the besieged people of Leyden, for poverty stood at the door, hunger and sickness were within, and no ship was anywhere seen coming to bring help. The father, who was a linen-weaver, could no longer work in the great factory; the mother, who was a lace-maker, had to leave her work to nurse him; and the old woman could earn only a trifle by her knitting, being lame and feeble. Little Trudel did what she could, — sold the stockings to get bread and medicine, picked up wood for the fire, gathered herbs for the poor soup, and ran errands for the market-women, who paid her with unsalable fruit, withered vegetables, and now and then a bit of meat.

But market-day came but once a week; and it was very hard to find food for the hungry mouths meantime. The Dorts were too proud to beg, so they suffered in silence, praying that help would come before it was too late to save the sick and old.

No other picture in the quaint book interested Trudel so much as that of the siege of Leyden; and she went back to it, thinking over the story till hunger made her look about for something to eat as eagerly as the poor starving burghers.

"Here, child, is a good crust. It is too hard for me. I kept it for you; it's the last except that bit for your mother," said the old woman, pulling a dry crust from her jacket with a smile; for though starving herself, the brave old soul thought only of her darling.

Trudel's little white teeth gnawed savagely at the hard bread, and Jan ate the crumbs as if he too needed food. As she saw him purring about her feet, there came into the child's head a sudden idea, born of the brave story and of the cares that made her old before her time.

"Poor Jan gets thinner and thinner every day. If we are to eat him, we must do it soon, or he will not be worth cooking," she said with a curious look on the face that used to be so round and rosy, and now was white, thin, and anxious.

"Bless the child! we won't eat the poor beast! but it would be kind to give him away to some one who could feed him well. Go now, dear, and get a jug of fresh water. The father will need it, and so will you, for that crust is a dry dinner for my darling."

As she spoke, the old woman held the little girl close for a minute; and Trudel clung to her silently, finding the help she needed for her sacrifice in the love and the example grandma gave her.

Then she ran away, with the brown jug in one hand, the pretty kitten on her arm, and courage in her little heart. It was a poor neighborhood where the weavers and lace-makers lived; but nearly every one had a good dinner on Sunday, and on her way to the fountain Trudel saw many well-spread tables, smelled the good soup in many kettles, and looked enviously at the plump children sitting quietly on the doorsteps in round caps and wooden shoes, waiting to be called in to eat of the big loaves, the brown sausages, and the cabbage-soup smoking on the hearth.

When she came to the baker's house, her heart began to beat; and she hugged Jan so close it was well he was thin, or he would have mewed under the tender farewell squeezes his little mistress gave him. With a timid hand Trudel knocked, and then went in to find Vrow Hertz and her five boys and girls at table, with good roast meat and bread and cheese and beer before them.

"Oh, the dear cat! the pretty cat! Let me pat him! Hear him mew, and see his soft white coat," cried the children, before Trudel could speak, for they admired the snow-white kitten very much, and had often begged for it.

Trudel had made up her mind to give up to them at last her one treasure; but she wished to be paid for it, and was bound to tell her plan. Jan helped her, for smelling the meat, he leaped from her arms to the table and began to gnaw a bone on Dirck's plate, which so amused the young people that they did not hear Trudel say to their mother in a low voice, with red cheeks and beseeching eyes, —

"Dear Vrow Hertz, the father is very ill; the

mother cannot work at her lace in the dark room; and grandma makes but little by knitting, though I help all I can. We have no food; can you give me a loaf of bread in exchange for Jan? I have nothing else to sell, and the children want him much."

Trudel's eyes were full and her lips trembled, as she ended with a look that went straight to stout Mother Hertz's kind heart, and told the whole sad story.

"Bless the dear child! Indeed, yes; a loaf and welcome; and see here, a good sausage also. Brenda, go fill the jug with milk. It is excellent for the sick man. As for the cat, let it stay a while and get fat, then we will see. It is a pretty beast and worth many loaves of bread; so come again, Trudel, and do not suffer hunger while I have much bread."

As the kind woman spoke, she had bustled about, and before Trudel could get her breath, a big loaf, a long sausage, and a jug of fresh milk were in her apron and hands, and a motherly kiss made the gifts all the easier to take. Returning it heartily, and telling the children to be kind to Jan, she hastened home to burst into the quiet room, crying joyfully, —

"See, grandmother, here is food, — all mine. I bought it! Come, come, and eat!"

"Now, dear Heaven, what do I see? Where did the blessed bread come from?" asked the old woman, hugging the big loaf, and eyeing the sausage with such hunger in her face that Trudel ran for the knife and cup, and held a draught of fresh milk to her grandmother's lips before she could answer a single question.

"Stay, child, let us give thanks before we eat. Never was food more welcome or hearts more grateful;" and folding her hands, the pious old woman blessed the meal that seemed to fall from heaven on that bare table. Then Trudel cut the crusty slice for herself, a large soft one for grandmother, with a good bit of sausage, and refilled the cup. Another portion and cup went upstairs to mother, whom she found asleep, with the father's hot hand in hers. So leaving the surprise for her waking, Trudel crept down to eat her own dinner, as hungry as a little wolf, amusing herself with making the old woman guess where and how she got this fine feast.

"This is our siege, grandmother; and we are eating Jan," she said at last, with the merriest laugh she had given for weeks.

"Eating Jan?" cried the old woman, staring at the sausage, as if for a moment she feared the kitten had been turned into that welcome shape by some miracle. Still laughing, Trudel told her story, and was well rewarded for her childish sacrifice by the look in grandmother's face as she said with a tender kiss, —

"Thou art a carrier-dove, my darling, coming home with good news and comfort under thy wing. God bless thee, my brave little heart, and grant that our siege be not a long one before help comes to us!"

Such a happy feast! and for dessert more kisses and praises for Trudel when the mother came down to hear the story and to tell how eagerly father had drank the fresh milk and gone to sleep again. Trudel was very well pleased with her bargain; but at night she missed Jan's soft purr for her lullaby, and cried herself to sleep, grieving for her lost pet, being only a child, after all, though trying to be a brave little woman for the sake of those she loved.

The big loaf and sausage took them nicely through the next day; but by Tuesday only crusts remained, and sorrel-soup, slightly flavored with the last scrap of sausage, was all they had to eat.

On Wednesday morning, Trudel had plaited her long yellow braids with care, smoothed down her one blue skirt, and put on her little black silk cap, making ready for the day's work. She was weak and hungry, but showed a bright face as she took her old basket and said, —

"Now I am off to market, grandmother, to sell the hose and get medicine and milk for father. I shall try to pick up something for dinner. The good neighbors often let me run errands for them, and give me a kuchen, a bit of cheese, or a taste of their nice coffee. I will bring you something, and come as soon as I can."

The old woman nodded and smiled, as she scoured the empty kettle till it shone, and watched the little figure trudge away with the big empty basket, and, she knew, with a still emptier little stomach. "Coffee!" sighed the grandmother; "one sip of the blessed drink would put life into me. When shall I ever taste it again?" and the poor soul sat down to her knitting with hands that trembled from weakness.

The Platz was a busy and a noisy scene when Trudel arrived, — for the thrifty Dutchwomen were early afoot; and stalls, carts, baskets, and cans were already arranged to make the most attractive display of fruit, vegetables, fish, cheese, butter, eggs, milk, and poultry, and the small wares country people came to buy.

Nodding and smiling, Trudel made her way

through the bustle to the booth where old Vrow Schmidt bought and sold the blue woollen hose that adorn the stout legs of young and old.

"Good-morning, child! I am glad to see thee and thy well-knit stockings, for I have orders for three pairs, and promised thy grandmother's, they are always so excellent," said the rosy-faced woman, as Trudel approached.

"I have but one pair. We had no money to buy more yarn. Father is so ill mother cannot work; and medicines cost a deal," said the child, with her large hungry eyes fixed on the breakfast the old woman was about to eat, first having made ready for the business of the day.

"See, then, I shall give thee the yarn and wait for the hose; I can trust thee, and shall ask a good price for the good work. Thou too wilt have the fever, I'm afraid! — so pale and thin, poor child! Here, drink from my cup, and take a bite of bread and cheese. The morning air makes one hungry."

Trudel eagerly accepted the "sup" and the "bite," and felt new strength flow into her as the warm draught and good brown bread went down her throat.

"So many thanks! I had no breakfast. I came to see if I could get any errands here to-day, for I want to earn a bit if I can," she said with a sigh of satisfaction, as she slipped half of her generous slice and a good bit of cheese into her basket, regretting that the coffee could not be shared also.

As if to answer her wish, a loud cry from fat Mother Kinkle, the fish-wife, rose at that moment, for a thievish cur had run off with a fish from her stall, while she gossiped with a neighbor.

Down went Trudel's basket, and away went Trudel's wooden shoes clattering over the stones while she raced after the dog, dodging in and out among the stalls till she cornered the thief under Gretchen Horn's milk-cart; for at sight of the big dog who drew the four copper-cans, the cur lost heart and dropped the fish and ran away.

"Well done!" said buxom Gretchen, when Trudel caught up the rescued treasure a good deal the worse for the dog's teeth and the dust it had been dragged through.

All the market-women laughed as the little girl came back proudly bearing the fish, for the race had amused them. But Mother Kinkle said with a sigh, when she saw the damage done her property, —

"It is spoiled; no one will buy that torn, dirty thing. Throw it on the muck-pile, child; your trouble was in vain, though I thank you for it."

"Give it to me, please, if you don't want it. We can eat it, and would be glad of it at home," cried Trudel, hugging the slippery fish with joy, for she saw a dinner in it, and felt that her run was well paid.

"Take it, then, and be off; I see Vrow von Decken's cook coming, and you are in the way," answered the old woman, who was not a very amiable person, as every one knew.

"That's a fine reward to make a child for running the breath out of her body for you," said Dame Troost, the handsome farm-wife who sat close by among her fruit and vegetables, as fresh as her cabbages, and as rosy as her cherries.

"Better it, then, and give her a feast fit for a burgomaster. *You* can afford it," growled Mother Kinkle, turning her back on the other woman in a huff.

"That I will, for very shame at such meanness! Here, child, take these for thy fish-stew, and these for thy little self," said the kind soul, throwing half a dozen potatoes and onions into the basket, and handing Trudel a cabbage-leaf full of cherries.

A happy girl was our little house-wife on her way home, when the milk and medicine and loaf of bread were bought; and a comfortable dinner was quickly cooked and gratefully eaten in Dort's poor house that day.

"Surely the saints must help you, child, and open people's hearts to our need; for you come back each day with food for us, — like the ravens to the people in the wilderness," said the grandmother when they sat at table.

"If they do, it is because you pray to them so heartily, mother. But I think the sweet ways and thin face of my Trudel do much to win kindness, and the good God makes her our little house-mother, while I must sit idle," answered Vrow Dort; and she filled the child's platter again that she, at least, might have enough.

"I like it!" cried Trudel, munching an onion with her bread, while her eyes shone and a pretty color came into her cheeks. "I feel so old and brave now, so glad to help; and things happen, and I keep thinking what I will do next to get food. It's like the birds out yonder in the hedge, trying to feed their little ones. I fly up and down, pick and scratch, get a bit here and a bit there, and then my dear *old* birds have food to eat."

It really was very much as Trudel said, for her small wits were getting very sharp with these new cares; she lay awake that night trying to plan how she should provide the next day's food for her family.

"Where now, thou dear little mother-bird?" asked the "Grossmutter" next morning, when the child had washed the last dish, and was setting away the remains of the loaf.

"To Gretti Jansen's, to see if she wants me to water her linen, as I used to do for play. She is lame, and it tires her to go to the spring so often. She will like me to help her, I hope; and I shall ask her for some food to pay me. Oh, I am very bold now! Soon will I beg if no other way offers." And Trudel shook her yellow head resolutely, and went to settle the stool at grandmother's feet, and to draw the curtain so that it would shield the old eyes from the summer sun.

"Heaven grant it never comes to that! It would be very hard to bear, yet perhaps we must if no help arrives. The doctor's bill, the rent, the good food thy father will soon need, will take far more than we can earn; and what will become of us, the saints only know!" answered the old woman, knitting briskly in spite of her sad forebodings.

"*I* will do it all! I don't know how, but I shall try; and, as you often say, 'Have faith and hold up thy hands; God will fill them.'"

Then Trudel went away to her work, with a stout heart under her little blue bodice; and all that summer day she trudged to and fro along the webs of linen spread in the green meadow, watering them as fast as they dried, knitting busily under a tree during the intervals.

Old Gretti was glad to have her, and at noon called her in to share the milk-soup, with cherries and herrings in it, and a pot of coffee, — as well as Dutch cheese, and bread full of coriander-seed. Though this was a feast to Trudel, one bowl of soup and a bit of bread was all she ate; then, with a face that was not half as "bold" as she tried to make it, she asked if she might run home and take the coffee to grandmother, who longed for and needed it so much.

"Yes, indeed; there, let me fill that pewter jug with a good hot mess for the old lady, and take this also. I have little to give, but I remember how good she was to me in the winter, when my poor legs were so bad, and no one else thought of me," said grateful Gretti, mixing more coffee, and tucking a bit of fresh butter into half a loaf of bread with a crusty end to cover the hole.

Away ran Trudel; and when grandmother saw the "blessed coffee," as she called it, she could only sip and sigh for comfort and content, so glad was the poor old soul to taste her favorite drink again. The mother smelled it, and came down to take her share, while Trudel skipped away to go on watering the linen till sunset with a happy heart, saying to herself while she trotted and splashed, —

"This day is well over, and I have kept my word. Now what *can* I do to-morrow? Gretti doesn't want me; there is no market; I must not beg yet, and I cannot finish the hose so soon.

"I know! I'll get water-cresses, and sell them from door to door. They are fresh now, and people like them. Ah, thou dear duck, thank thee for reminding me of them," she cried, as she watched a mother-duck lead her brood along the brook's edge, picking and dabbling among the weeds to show them where to feed.

Early next morning Trudel took her basket and went away to the meadows that lay just out of the town, where the rich folk had their summer houses, and fish-ponds, and gardens. These gardens were gay now with tulips, the delight of Dutch people; for they know best how to cultivate them, and often make fortunes out of the splendid and costly flowers.

When Trudel had looked long and carefully for

cresses, and found very few, she sat down to rest, weary and disappointed, on a green bank from which she could overlook a fine garden all ablaze with tulips. She admired them heartily, longed to have a bed of them for her own, and feasted her childish eyes on the brilliant colors till they were dazzled, for the long beds of purple and yellow, red and white blossoms were splendid to see, and in the midst of all a mound of dragon-tulips rose like a queen's throne, scarlet, green, and gold all mingled on the ruffled leaves that waved in the wind.

Suddenly it seemed as if one of the great flowers had blown over the wall and was hopping along the path in a very curious way! In a minute, however, she saw that it was a gay parrot that had escaped, and would have flown away if its clipped wings and a broken chain on one leg had not kept it down.

Trudel laughed to see the bird scuttle along, jabbering to itself, and looking very mischievous and naughty as it ran away. She was just thinking she ought to stop it, when the garden-gate opened, and a pretty little boy came out, calling anxiously, —

"Prince! Prince! Come back, you bad bird! I never will let you off your perch again, sly rascal!"

"I will get him!" and Trudel ran down the bank

after the runaway, for the lad was small and leaned upon a little crutch.

"Be careful! He will bite," called the boy.

"I'm not afraid," answered Trudel; and she stepped on the chain, which brought the "Prince of Orange" to a very undignified and sudden halt. But when she tried to catch him up by his legs, the sharp black beak gave a nip and held tightly to her arm. It hurt her much, but she did not let go, and carried her captive back to its master, who thanked her, and begged her to come in and chain up the bad bird, for he was evidently rather afraid of it.

Glad to see more of the splendid garden, Trudel did what he asked, and with a good deal of fluttering, scolding, and pecking, the Prince was again settled on his perch.

"Your arm is bleeding! Let me tie it up for you; and here is my cake to pay you for helping me. Mamma would have been very angry if Prince had been lost," said the boy, as he wet his little handkerchief in a tank of water near by, and tied up Trudel's arm.

The tank was surrounded by pots of tulips; and on a rustic seat lay the lad's hat and a delicious large kuchen, covered with comfits and sugar. The hungry girl accepted it gladly, but only nibbled at it, remembering those at home. The boy thought she did not like it, and being a generous little fellow and very grateful for her help, he looked about for something else to give her. Seeing her eyes fixed admiringly on a pretty red jar that held a dragon-tulip just ready to bloom, he said pleasantly, —

"Would you like this also? All these are mine, and I can do as I like with them. Will you have it?"

"Oh, yes, with thanks! It is *so* beautiful! I longed for one, but never thought to get it," cried Trudel, receiving the pot with delight.

Then she hastened toward home to show her prize, only stopping to sell her little bunches of cresses for a few groschen, with which she bought a loaf and three herrings to eat with it. The cake and the flower gave quite the air of a feast to the poor meal, but Trudel and the two women enjoyed it all, for the doctor said that the father was better, and now needed only good meat and wine to grow strong and well again.

How to get these costly things no one knew, but trusted they would come, and all fell to work with lighter hearts. The mother sat again at her lace-work, for now a ray of light could be allowed to fall on her pillow and bobbins by the window of the sick-room. The old woman's fingers flew as she knit at one long blue stocking; and Trudel's little hands tugged away at the other, while she cheered her dull task by looking fondly at her dear tulip unfolding in the sun.

She began to knit next day as soon as the breakfast of dry bread and water was done; but she took her work to the doorstep and thought busily as the needles clicked, for where *could* she get money enough for meat and wine? The pretty pot stood beside her, and the tulip showed its gay leaves now, just ready to bloom. She was very proud of it, and smiled and nodded gayly when a neighbor said in passing, "A fine flower you have there."

Soon she forgot it, however, so hard was her little brain at work, and for a long time she sat with her eyes fixed on her busy hands so intently that she neither heard steps approaching, nor saw a maid and a little girl looking over the low fence at her. Suddenly some words in a strange language made her look up. The child was pointing at the tulip and talking fast in English to the maid, who shook her head and tried to lead her on.

She was a pretty little creature, all in white with a gay hat, curly locks, and a great doll in one arm, while the other held a box of bonbons. Trudel smiled when she saw the doll; and as if the friendly look decided her, the little girl ran up to the door, pointed to the flower, and asked a question in the queer tongue which Trudel could not understand. The maid followed, and said in Dutch, "Fräulein Maud wishes the flower. Will you give it to her, child?"

"Oh, no, no! I love it. I will keep it, for now Jan is gone, it is all I have!" answered Trudel, taking the pot in her lap to guard her one treasure.

The child frowned, chattered eagerly, and offered the box of sweets, as if used to having her wishes gratified at once. But Trudel shook her head, for much as she loved "sugar-drops," she loved the splendid flower better, like a true little Dutchwoman.

Then Miss Maud offered the doll, bent on having her own way. Trudel hesitated a moment, for the fine lady doll in pink silk, with a feather in her hat, and tiny shoes on her feet, was very tempting to her childish soul. But she felt that so dainty a thing was not for her, and her old wooden darling, with the staring eyes and broken nose, was dearer to her than the delicate stranger could ever be. So she smiled to soothe the disappointed child, but shook her head again.

At that, the English lassie lost her temper,

stamped her foot, scolded, and began to cry, ordering the maid to take the flower and come away at once.

"She *will* have it; and she must not cry. Here, child, will you sell it for this?" said the maid, pulling a handful of groschen out of her deep pocket, sure that Trudel would yield now.

But the little house-mother's quick eye saw that the whole handful would not buy the meat and wine, much as it looked, and for the third time she shook her yellow head. There was a longing look in her face, however; and the shrewd maid saw it, guessed that money would win the day, and diving again into her apron-pocket, brought out a silver gulden and held it up.

"For this, then, little miser? It is more than the silly flower is worth; but the young fräulein must have all she wants, so take it and let us be done with the crying."

A struggle went on in Trudel's mind; and for a moment she did not speak. She longed to keep her dear tulip, her one joy, and it seemed so hard to let it go before she had even seen it blossom once; but then the money would do much, and her loving little heart yearned to give poor father all he needed. Just then her mother's voice came down from the open window, softly singing an old hymn to lull the sick man to sleep. That settled the matter for the dutiful daughter; tears rose to her eyes, and she found it very hard to say with a farewell caress of the blue and yellow pot as she gave it up, —

"You may have it; but it *is* worth more than a gulden, for it is a dragon-tulip, the finest we have. Could you give a little more? my father is very sick, and we are very poor."

The stout maid had a kind heart under her white muslin neckerchief; and while Miss Maud seized the flower, good Marta put another gulden into Trudel's hand before she hastened after her charge, who made off with her booty, as if fearing to lose it.

Trudel watched the child with the half-opened tulip nodding over her shoulder, as though it sadly said "good-by" to its former mistress, till her dim eyes could see no longer. Then she covered her face with her apron and sobbed very quietly, lest grandmother should hear and be troubled. But Trudel was a brave child, and soon the tears stopped, the blue eyes looked gladly at the money in her hand, and presently, when the fresh wind had cooled her cheeks, she went in to show her treasure and cheer up the anxious hearts with her good news.

She made light of the loss of her flower, and still

knitting, went briskly off to get the meat and wine for father, and if the money held out, some coffee for grandmother, some eggs and white rolls for mother, who was weak and worn with her long nursing.

"Surely, the dear God does help me," thought the pious little maid, while she trudged back with her parcels, quite cheery again, though no pretty kitten ran to meet her, and no gay tulip stood full-blown in the noonday sun.

Still more happy was she over her small sacrifices when she saw her father sip a little of the good broth grandmother made with such care, and saw the color come into the pale cheeks of the dear mother after she had taken the eggs and fine bread, with a cup of coffee to strengthen and refresh her.

"We have enough for to-day, and for father to-morrow; but on Sunday we must fast as well as pray, unless the hose be done and paid for in time," said the old woman next morning, surveying their small store of food with an anxious eye.

"I will work hard, and go to Vrow Schmidt's the minute we are done. But now I must run and get wood, else the broth will not be ready," answered Trudel, clattering on her wooden shoes in a great hurry.

"If all else fails, I too shall make my sacrifice as well as you, my heart's darling. I cannot knit as I once did, and if we are not done, or Vrow Schmidt be away, I will sell my ring and so feed the flock till Monday," said the grandmother, lifting up one thin old hand, where shone the wedding-ring she had worn so many years.

"Ah, no,— not that! It was so sad to see your gold beads go, and mother's ear-rings and father's coat and Jan and my lovely flower! We will not sell the dear old ring. I will find a way. Something will happen, as before; so wait a little, and trust to me," cried Trudel, with her arms about her grandmother, and such a resolute nod that the rusty little black cap fell over her nose and extinguished her.

She laughed as she righted it, and went singing away, as if not a care lay heavy on her young heart. But when she came to the long dike which kept the waters of the lake from overflowing the fields below, she walked slowly to rest her tired legs, and to refresh her eyes with the blue sheet of water on one side and the still bluer flax-fields on the other, — for they were in full bloom, and the delicate flowers danced like fairies in the wind.

It was a lonely place, but Trudel liked it, and

went on toward the wood, turning the heel of her stocking while she walked, — pausing now and then to look over at the sluice-gates which stood here and there ready to let off the water when autumn rains made the lake rise, or in the spring when the flax-fields were overflowed before the seed was sown. At the last of these she paused to gather a bunch of yellow stone-crop growing from a niche in the strong wall which, with earth and beams, made the dike. As she stooped, the sound of voices in the arch below came up to her distinctly. Few people came that way except little girls, like herself, to gather fagots in the wood, or truant lads to fish in the pond. Thinking the hidden speakers must be some of these boys, she knelt down behind the shrubs that grew along the banks, and listened with a smile on her lips to hear what mischief the naughty fellows were planning. But the smile soon changed to a look of terror; and she crouched low behind the bushes to catch all that was said in the echoing arch below.

"How did I think of the thing? Why, that is the best part of the joke! Mein Herr von Vost put it into my head himself," said a man's gruff voice, in answer to some question. "This is the way it was: I sat at the window of the beer-house, and Von Vost met the burgomaster close by and said, 'My friend, I hear that the lower sluice-gate needs looking to. Please see to it speedily, for an overflow now would ruin my flax-fields, and cause many of my looms to stand still next winter.' 'So! It shall be looked to next week. Such a misfortune shall not befall you, my good neighbor,' said the burgomaster; and they parted. 'Ah, ha!' thinks I to myself, 'here we have a fine way to revenge ourselves on Master von Vost, who turned us off and leaves us to starve. We have but to see that the old gate gives way *between* now and *Monday*, and that hard man will suffer in the only place where he *can* feel, — his pocket.' "

Here the gruff voice broke into a low laugh, and another man said slowly, —

"A good plan; but is there no danger of being found out, Peit Stensen?"

"Not a chance of it! See here, Deitrich, a quiet blow or two, at night when none can hear it, will break away these rotten boards and let the water in. The rest — it will do itself; and by morning those great fields will be many feet under water, and Von Vost's crop ruined. Yes, we *will* stop his looms for him, and other men besides you and I and Niklas Haas will stand idle with starving children round them. Come, will you lend a hand?

Niklas is away looking for work, and Hans Dort is sick, or they might be glad to help us."

"Hans would never do it. He is sober, and so good a weaver he will never want work when he is well. I *will* be with you, Peit; but swear not to tell it, whatever happens, for you and I have bad names now, and it would go hard with us."

"I'll swear anything; but have no fear. We will not only be revenged on the master, but get the job of repairing; since men are scarce and the need will be great when the flood is discovered. See, then, how fine a plan it is! and meet me here at twelve tonight with a shovel and pick. Mine are already hidden in the wood yonder. Now, come and see where we must strike, and then slip home the other way; we must not be seen here by any one."

There the voices stopped, and steps were heard going deeper into the arch. Trudel, pale with fear, rose to her feet, slipped off her sabots, and ran away along the dike like a startled rabbit, never pausing till she was safely round the corner and out of sight. Then she took breath, and tried to think what to do first. It was of no use to go home and tell the story there. Father was too ill to hear it or to help; and if she told the neighbors, the secret would soon be known everywhere and might bring danger on them all. No, she must go at once to Mein Herr von Vost and tell him alone, begging him to let no one know what she had heard, but to prevent the mischief the men threatened, as if by accident. Then all would be safe, and the pretty flax-fields kept from drowning. It was a long way to the "master's," as he was called, because he owned the linen factories, where all day many looms jangled, and many men and women worked busily to fill his warehouses and ships with piles of the fine white cloth, famous all the world over.

But forgetting the wood, father's broth, granny's coffee, and even the knitting which she still held, Trudel went as fast as she could toward the country-house, where Mein Herr von Vost would probably be at his breakfast.

She was faint now with hunger and heat, for the day grew hot, and the anxiety she felt made her heart flutter while she hurried along the dusty road till she came to the pretty house in its gay garden, where some children were playing. Anxious not to be seen, Trudel slipped up the steps, and in at the open window of a room where she saw the master and his wife sitting at table. Both looked surprised to see a shabby, breathless little girl enter in that curious fashion; but something in her face told them that she came on an important errand, and putting down his cup, the gentleman said quickly, —

"Well, girl, what is it?"

In a few words Trudel told her story, adding with a beseeching gesture, "Dear sir, please do not tell that I betrayed bad Peit and Deitrich. They know father, and may do him some harm if they discover that I told you this. We are so poor, so unhappy now, we cannot bear any more;" and quite overcome with the troubles that filled her little heart, and the fatigue and the hunger that weakened her little body, Trudel dropped down at Von Vost's feet as if she were dead.

When she came to herself, she was lying on a velvet sofa and the sweet-faced lady was holding wine to her lips, while Mein Herr von Vost marched up and down the room with his flowered dressing-gown waving behind him, and a frown on his brow. Trudel sat up and said she was quite well; but the little white face and the hungry eyes that wandered to the breakfast-table, told the truth, and the good frau had a plate of food and a cup of warm milk before her in a moment.

"Eat, my poor child, and rest a little, while the master considers what is best to be done, and how to reward the brave little messenger who came so far to save his property," said the motherly lady, fanning Trudel, who ate heartily, hardly knowing what she ate, except that it was very delicious after so much bread and water.

In a few moments Herr von Vost paused before the sofa and said kindly, though his eyes were stern and his face looked hard, —

"See, then, thus shall I arrange the affair, and all will be well. I will myself go to see the old gate, as if made anxious lest the burgomaster should forget his promise. I find it in a dangerous state, and at once set my men at work. The rascals are disappointed of both revenge and wages, and I can soon take care of them in other ways, for they are drunken fellows, and are easily clapped into prison and kept safely there till ready to work and to stop plotting mischief. No one shall know your part in it, my girl; but I do not forget it. Tell your father his loom waits for him. Meanwhile, here is something to help while he must be idle."

Trudel's plate nearly fell out of her hands as a great gold-piece dropped into her lap; and she could only stammer her thanks with tears of joy, and a mouth full of bread and butter.

"He is a kind man, but a busy one, and people call him 'hard.' *You* will not find him so hereafter, for he never forgets a favor, nor do I. Eat well, dear child, and wait till you are rested. I will get a basket of comforts for the sick man. Who else needs help at home?"

So kindly did Frau von Vost look and speak that Trudel told all her sad tale freely, for the master had gone at once to see to the dike, after a nod and a pat on the child's head, which made her quite sure that he was not as hard as people said.

When she had opened her heart to the friendly lady, Trudel was left to rest a few moments, and lay luxuriously on the yellow sofa staring at the handsome things about her, and eating pretzels till Frau von Vost returned with the promised basket, out of which peeped the neck of a wine-bottle, the legs of a chicken, glimpses of grapes, and many neat parcels of good things.

"My servant goes to market and will carry this for you till you are near home. Go, little Trudel; and God bless you for saving us from a great misfortune!" said the lady; and she kissed the happy child and led her to the back door, where stood the little cart with an old man to drive the fat horse, and many baskets to be filled in town.

Such a lovely drive our Trudel had that day! No queen in a splendid chariot ever felt prouder, for all her cares were gone, gold was in her pocket, food at her feet, and friends secured to make times easier for all. No need to tell how joyfully she was welcomed at home, nor what praises she received when her secret was confided to mother and grandmother, nor what a feast was spread in the poor house that day, — for patience, courage, and trust in God had won the battle, the enemy had fled, and Trudel's hard siege was over.

MUSIC AND MACARONI

AMONG the pretty villages that lie along the wonderful Cornice road which runs from Nice to Genoa, none was more beautiful than Valrose. It deserved its fame, for it was indeed a "valley of roses." The little town with its old church nestled among the olive and orange trees that clothed the hillside, sloping up to purple mountains towering behind. Lower down stretched the vineyards; and the valley was a bed of flowers all the year round. There were acres of violets, verbenas, mignonette, and every sweet-scented blossom that grows, while hedges of roses, and valleys of lemon-trees with their white stars made the air heavy with perfume. Across the plain, one saw the blue sea rolling to meet the bluer sky, sending fresh airs and soft rains to keep Valrose green and beautiful even through the summer heat. Only one ugly thing marred the lovely landscape, and that was the factory, with its tall chimneys, its red walls, and ceaseless bustle. But old ilex-trees tried to conceal its ugliness; the smoke curled gracefully from its chimney-tops; and the brown men talked in their musical language as they ran about the busy courtyard, or did strange things below in the still-room. Handsome black-eyed girls sang at the open windows at their pretty work, and delicious odors filled the place; for here the flowers that bloomed outside were changed to all kinds of delicate perfumes to scent the hair of great ladies and the handkerchiefs of dainty gentlemen all the world over.

The poor roses, violets, mignonette, orange-flowers, and their sisters, were brought here in great baskets to yield up their sweet souls in hot rooms where fires burned and great vats boiled; then they were sent up to be imprisoned in pretty flasks of all imaginable shapes and colors by the girls, who put gilded labels on them, packed them in delicate boxes, and sent them away to comfort the sick, please the rich, and put money in the pockets of the merchants.

Many children were employed in the light work of weeding beds, gathering flowers, and running errands; among these none were busier, happier, or more beloved than Florentino and his sister Stella. They were orphans, but they lived with old Mariuccia in her little stone house near the church, contented with the small wages they earned, though their clothes were poor, their food salad, macaroni, rye bread, and thin wine, with now and then a taste of meat when Stella's lover or some richer friend gave them a treat on gala days.

They worked hard, and had their dreams of what they would do when they had saved up a little store; Stella would marry her Beppo and settle in a home of her own; but Tino was more ambitious, for he possessed a sweet boyish voice and sang so well in the choir, at the merry-makings, and about his work, that he was called the "little nightingale," and much praised and petted, not only by his mates, but by the good priest who taught him music, and the travellers who often came to the factory and were not allowed to go till Tino had sung to them.

All this made the lad vain; and he hoped one day to go away as Baptista had gone, who now sang in a fine church at Genoa and sent home gold napoleons to his old parents. How this was to come about Tino had not the least idea, but he cheered his work with all manner of wild plans, and sang his best at Mass, hoping some stranger would hear, and take him away as Signor Pulci had taken big Tista, whose voice was not half so wonderful as his own, all had said. No one came, however, and Tino at thirteen was still at work in the valley, — a happy little lad, singing all day long as he carried his fragrant loads to and fro, ate his dinner of bread and beans fried in oil, with a crust, under the ilex-trees, and slept like a dormouse at night on his clean straw in the loft at Mariuccia's, with the moon for his candle and the summer warmth for his coverlet.

One day in September, as he stood winnowing mignonette seed in a quiet corner of the vast garden, he was thinking deeply over his hopes and plans, and practising the last chant Father Angelo had taught him, while he shook and held the sieve high, to let the wind blow away the dead husks, leaving the brown seeds behind.

Suddenly, as he ended his lesson with a clear high note that seemed to rise and die softly away like the voice of an angel in the air, the sound of applause startled him; and turning, he saw a gentleman sitting on the rude bench behind him, — a well-dressed, handsome, smiling gentleman, who clapped his white hands and nodded and said gayly, "Bravo, my boy, that was well done! You have a wonderful voice; sing again."

But Tino was too abashed for the moment, and could only stand and stare at the stranger, a pretty picture of boyish confusion, pleasure, and shyness.

"Come, tell me all about it, my friend. Who taught you so well? Why are you here, and not where you should be learning to use this fine pipe of yours, and make fame and money by it?" said the gentleman, still smiling as he leaned easily in his seat and swung his gloves.

Tino's heart began to beat fast as he thought, "Perhaps my chance has come at last! I must make the most of it." So taking courage, he told his little story; and when he ended, the stranger gave a nod, saying, —

"Yes, you are the 'little nightingale' they spoke of up at the inn. I came to find you. Now sing me something gay, some of your folk-songs. That sort will suit you best."

Anxious to make the most of his chance, Tino took courage and sang away as easily as a bird on a bough, pouring out one after another the barcaroles, serenades, ballads, and drinking-songs he had learned from the people about him.

The gentleman listened, laughed, and applauded as if well pleased, and when Tino stopped to take breath, he gave another nod more decided than the first, and said with his engaging smile, —

"You are indeed a wonder, and quite wasted here. If *I* had you, I should make a man of you, and put money in your pocket as fast as you opened your mouth."

Tino's eyes sparkled at the word "money," for

sweet as was the praise, the idea of having full pockets bewitched him, and he asked eagerly, "How, signor?"

"Well," answered the gentleman, idly tapping his nose with a rose-bud which he had pulled as he came along, "I should take you to my hotel at Nice; wash, brush, and trim you up a little; put you into a velvet suit with a lace collar, silk stockings, and buckled shoes; teach you music, feed you well, and when I thought you fit, carry you with me to the *salons* of the great people, where I give concerts. There you would sing these gay songs of yours, and be petted, praised, and pelted with bonbons, francs, and kisses perhaps, — for you are a pretty lad and these fine ladies and idle gentlemen are always ready to welcome a new favorite. Would you fancy that sort of life better than this? You can have it if you like."

Tino's black eyes shone; the color deepened in his brown cheeks; and he showed all his white teeth as he laughed and exclaimed with a gesture of delight, —

"Mio Dio! but I *would*, signor! I'm tired of this work; I long to sing, to see the world, to be my own master, and let Stella and the old woman know that I am big enough to have my own way. Do you really mean it? When can I go? I'm ready now, only I had better run and put on my holiday suit and get my guitar."

"Good! there's a lad of spirit. I like that well. A guitar, too? Bravo, my little troubadour, we shall make a sensation in the drawing-rooms, and fill our pockets shortly. But there is no haste, and it would be well to ask these friends of yours, or there might be trouble. I don't *steal* nightingales, I buy them; and I will give the old woman, whoever she may be, more than you would earn in a month. See, I too am a singer, and this I made at Genoa in a week." As he spoke, Signor Mario pulled a well-filled purse from one pocket, a handful of gold and silver coin from the other, and chinked them before the boy's admiring eyes.

"Let us go!" cried Tino, flinging down the sieve as if done with work forever. "Stella is at home to-day; come at once to Mariuccia, — it is not far; and when they hear these fine plans, they will be glad to let me go, I am sure."

Away he went across the field of flowers, through the courtyard, up the steep street, straight into the kitchen where his pretty sister sat eating artichokes and bread while the old woman twirled her distaff in the sun. Both were used to strangers, for the cottage was a picturesque place, half hidden like a bird's nest in vines and fig-trees, with a gay little plot of flowers before it; travellers often came to taste Mariuccia's honey, for her bees fared well, and their combs were running over with the sweetness of violets and roses, put up in dainty little waxen boxes made by better workmen than any found at the factory.

The two women listened respectfully while Signor Mario told his plan in his delightfully gracious way; and Stella was much impressed by the splendor of the prospect before her brother. But the wise old woman shook her head, and declared decidedly that the boy was too young to leave home yet. Father Angelo was teaching him well; he was safe and happy where he was; and there he should remain, for she had sworn by all the saints to his dying mother that she would guard him as the apple of her eye till he was old enough to take care of himself.

In vain Mario shook his purse before her eyes, Stella pleaded, and Tino stormed; the faithful old soul would not give up, much as she needed money, loved Stella, and hated to cross the boy who was in truth "the apple of her eye" and the darling of her heart. There was a lively scene in the little room, for every one talked at once, gesticulated wildly, and grew much excited in the discussion; but nothing came of it, and Signor Mario departed wrathfully, leaving Mariuccia looking as stern as fate with her distaff, Stella in tears, and Tino in such a rage he could only dash up to the loft and throw himself on his rude bed, there to kick and sob and tear his hair, and wish there might be ten thousand earthquakes to swallow that cruel old woman up in the twinkling of an eye.

Stella came to beg him to be comforted and eat his supper, but he drew the wooden bolt and would not let her in, saying sternly, —

"I *never* will come down till Mariuccia says I may go; I will starve first. I am not a child to be so treated. Go away, and let me alone; I hate you both!"

Poor Stella retired, heart-broken, and when all her entreaties failed to change their guardian's decision, she went to consult Father Angelo. He agreed with the old woman that it was best to keep the boy safe at home, as they knew nothing of the strange gentleman nor what might befall Tino if he left the shelter of his own humble home and friends.

Much disappointed, Stella went to pray devoutly

in the church, and then, meeting her Beppo, soon forgot all about the poor little lad who had sobbed himself to sleep upon his straw.

The house was quiet when he awoke; no lights shone from any neighbor's windows; and all was still except the nightingales singing in the valley. The moon was up; and her friendly face looked in at the little window so brightly that the boy felt comforted, and lay staring at the soft light while his mind worked busily. Some evil spirit, some naughty Puck bent on mischief must have been abroad that night, for into Tino's head there suddenly popped a splendid idea; at least *he* thought it so, and in his rebellious state found it all the more tempting because danger and disobedience and defiance all had a part in it.

Why not run away? Signor Mario was not to leave till next morning. Tino could easily slip out early and join the kind gentleman beyond the town. This would show the women that he, Tino, had a will of his own and was not to be treated like a child any more. It would give them a good fright, make a fine stir in the place, and add to his glory when he returned with plenty of money to display himself in the velvet suit and silk stockings, — a famous fellow who knew what he was about and did not mean to be insulted, or tied to an old woman's apron-string forever.

The longer he thought the more delightful the idea became, and he resolved to carry it out, for the fine tales he had heard made him more discontented than ever with his present simple, care-free life. Up he got, and by the light of the moon took from the old chest his best suit. Moving very softly, he put on the breeches and jacket of rough blue cloth, the coarse linen shirt, the red sash, and the sandals of russet leather that laced about his legs to the knee. A few clothes, with his rosary, he tied up in a handkerchief, and laid the little bundle ready with his Sunday hat, a broad-brimmed, pointed-crowned affair with a red band and cock's feather to adorn it.

Then he sat at the window waiting for dawn to come, fearing to sleep lest he be too late. It seemed an almost endless night, the first he had ever spent awake, but red streaks came in the east at last, and he stole to the door, meaning to creep noiselessly downstairs, take a good hunch of bread and a gourd full of wine and slip off while the women slept.

To his dismay he found the door barred on the outside. His courage had ebbed a little as the time for action came; but at this new insult he got angry again, and every dutiful impulse flew away in a minute.

"Ah, they think to keep me, do they? Behold, then, how I cheat the silly things! They have never seen me climb down the fig-tree, and thought me safe. Now I will vanish, and leave them to tear their hair and weep for me in vain."

Flinging out his bundle, and carefully lowering his old guitar, Tino leaned from the little window, caught the nearest branch of the tree that bent toward the wall, and swung himself down as nimbly as a squirrel. Pausing only to pick several bunches of ripe grapes from the vine about the door, he went softly through the garden and ran away along the road toward Nice as fast as his legs could carry him.

Not till he reached the top of the long hill a mile away, did he slacken his lively pace; then climbing a bank, he lay down to rest under some olive-trees, and ate his grapes as he watched the sun rise. Travellers always left the Falcone Inn early to enjoy the morning freshness, so Tino knew that Signor Mario would soon appear; and when the horses paused to rest on the hill-top, the "little nightingale" would present himself as unexpectedly as if he had fallen from heaven.

But Signor Mario was a lazy man; and Tino had

time to work himself into a fever of expectation, doubt, and fear before the roll of wheels greeted his longing ears. Yes, it was the delightful stranger! — reading papers and smoking as he rode, quite blind to the beauty all around him, blind also to the sudden appearance of a picturesque little figure by the roadside, as the carriage stopped. Even when he looked, he did not recognize shabby Tino in the well-dressed beggar, as he thought him, who stood bare-headed and smiling, with hat in one hand, bundle in the other, and guitar slung on his back. He waved his hand as if to say, "I have nothing for you," and was about to bid the man drive on, but Tino cried out boldly, —

"Behold me, signor! I am Tino, the singing boy of Valrose. I have run away to join you if you will have me. Ah, please do! I wish so much to go with you."

"Bravo!" cried Mario, well pleased. "That is a lad of spirit; and I am glad to have you. I don't steal nightingales, as I told you down yonder; but if they get out of their cages and perch on my finger, I keep them. In with you, boy! there is no time to lose."

In scrambled happy Tino, and settling himself and his property on the seat opposite, amused his new master with a lively account of his escape.

Music and Macaroni 199

Mario laughed and praised him; Luigi, the servant, grinned as he listened from the coach-box; and the driver resolved to tell the tale at the Falcone, when he stopped there on his return to Genoa, so the lad's friends might know what had become of him.

After a little chat Signor Mario returned to his newspapers, and Tino, tired with his long vigil and brisk run, curled himself up on the seat, pillowed his head on his bundle and fell fast asleep, rocked by the motion of the carriage as it rolled along the smooth road.

When he waked, the sun was high, the carriage stood before a wayside inn, the man and horses were gone to their dinners, and the signor lay under some mulberry-trees in the garden while Luigi set forth upon the grass the contents of a well-filled hamper which they had brought with them, his master being one who looked well after his own comfort. The sight of food drew Tino toward it as straight as a honey-jar draws flies, and he presented himself with his most engaging air. Being in a good humor, the new master bade the hungry lad sit down and eat, which he did so heartily that larded fowl, melon, wine, and bread vanished as if by magic. Never had food tasted so good to Tino; and rejoicing with true boyish delight in the prospect of plenty to eat, he went off to play Morso with the driver, while the horses rested and Mario took a siesta on the grass.

When they set forth again, Tino received his first music lesson from the new teacher, who was well pleased to find how quickly the boy caught the air of a Venetian boat-song, and how sweetly he sang it. Then Tino strummed on his guitar and amused his hearers with all the melodies he knew, from church chants to drinking-songs. Mario taught him how to handle his instrument gracefully, speak a few polite phrases, and sit properly instead of sprawling awkwardly or lounging idly.

So the afternoon wore away; and at dusk they reached Nice. To Tino it looked like an enchanted city as they drove down to it from the soft gloom and stillness of the country. The sea broke gently on the curving shore, sparkling with the lights of the Promenade des Anglais which overlooks it. A half circle of brilliant hotels came next; behind these the glimmer of villas scattered along the hillside shone like fire-flies among gardens and orange groves; and higher still the stars burned in a violet sky. Soon the moon would be up, to hang like a great lamp from that splendid dome, turning sea and shore to a magic world by her light. Tino clapped his hands and looked about him with all the pleasure of his beauty-loving race as they rattled through the gay streets and stopped at one of the fine hotels.

Here Mario put on his grand air, and was shown to the apartment he had ordered from Genoa. Tino meekly followed; and Luigi brought up the rear with the luggage. Tino felt as if he had got into a fairy tale when he found himself in a fine parlor where he could only sit and stare about him, while his master refreshed in the chamber beyond, and the man ordered dinner. A large closet was given the boy to sleep in, with a mattress and blanket, a basin and pitcher, and a few pegs to hang his clothes on. But it seemed very nice after the loft; and when he had washed his face, shaken the dust off, and smoothed his curly head as well as he could, he returned to the parlor to gloat over such a dinner as he had never eaten before.

Mario was in a good humor and anxious to keep the lad so, therefore he plied him with good things to eat, fine promises, and the praise in which that vain little soul delighted. Tino went to bed early, feeling that his fortune was made, and his master went off to amuse himself at a gaming-table, for that was his favorite pastime.

Next day the new life began. After a late breakfast, a music lesson was given which both interested and dismayed Tino, for his master was far less patient than good old Father Angelo, and swore at him when he failed to catch a new air as quickly as he expected. Both were tired and rather cross when it ended, but Tino soon forgot the tweaking of his ear and the scolding, when he was sent away with Luigi to buy the velvet suit and sundry necessary articles for the young troubadour.

It was a lovely day; and the gay city was all alive with the picturesque bustle which always fills it when the season begins. Red-capped fishermen were launching their boats from the beach, flower-girls hastening from the gardens with their fragrant loads to sell on the Promenade, where invalids sunned themselves, nurses led their rosy troops to play, fine ladies strolled, and men of all nations paced to and fro at certain hours. In the older part of the city, work of all sorts went on, — coral-carvers filled their windows with pretty ornaments; pastry-cooks tempted with dainty dishes; milliners showed hats fresh from Paris; and Turkish merchants hung out rich rugs and carpets at their doors. Church-bells chimed; priests with incense and banners went through the streets on holy errands; the Pifferoni piped gayly; orange-women and chestnut-sellers called their wares in musical voices; even the little scullions who go about scouring saucepans at back doors made a song of their cry, "Casserola!"

Tino had a charming time, and could hardly believe his senses when one fine thing after another was bought for him and ordered home. Not only the suit, but two ruffled shirts, a crimson tie for the lace collar, a broad new ribbon for the guitar, handkerchiefs, hose, and delicate shoes, as if he was a gentleman's son. When Luigi added a little mantle and a hat such as other well-dressed lads of his age wore, Tino exclaimed, "This also! Dio mio, never have I known so kind a man as Signor Mario. I shall serve him well and love him even better than you do."

Luigi shrugged his shoulders and answered with a disagreeable laugh, "Long may you think so, poverino; I serve for money, not love, and look to it that I get my wages, else it would go ill with both of us. Keep all you can get, boy; our master is apt to forget his servants."

Tino did not like the look, half scornful, half pitiful, which Luigi gave him, and wondered why he did not love the good signor. Later he found out; but all was pleasant now, and lunch at a café completed the delights of that long morning.

The rooms were empty when they returned; and

bidding him keep out of mischief, Luigi left Tino alone for several hours. But he found plenty of amusement in examining all the wonders the apartment contained, receiving the precious parcels as they arrived, practising his new bow before the long mirror, and eating the nuts that he had bought of a jolly old woman at a street corner.

Then he went to lounge on the balcony that ran along the front of the hotel, and watched the lively scene below, till sunset sent the promenaders home to dress for dinner. Feeling a sudden pang of homesickness as he thought of Stella, Tino got his guitar and sang the old songs to comfort his loneliness.

The first was hardly ended before one after the other five little heads popped out of a window farther down the balcony; and presently a group of pretty children were listening and smiling as the nice boy played and sang to them. A gentleman looked out; and a lady evidently listened, for the end of a lace flounce lay on the threshold of the long window, and a pair of white hands clapped when he finished a gay air in his best style.

This was his first taste of applause, and he liked it, and twanged away merrily till his master's voice called him in just as he was beginning to answer the questions the eager children asked him.

"Go and dress! I shall take you down to dinner with me presently. But mind this, *I* will answer questions; do *you* keep quiet, and leave me to tell what I think best. Remember, or I pack you home at once."

Tino promised, and was soon absorbed in getting into his new clothes; Luigi came to help him, and when he was finished off, a very handsome lad emerged from the closet to make his best bow to his master, who, also in fine array, surveyed him with entire approval.

"Very good! I thought you would make a passable butterfly when you shed your grub's skin. Stand up and keep your hands out of your pockets. Mind what I told you about supping soup noisily, and don't handle your fork like a shovel. See what others do, smile, and hold your tongue. There is the gong. Let us go."

Tino's heart beat as he followed Mario down the long hall to the great *salle à manger* with its glittering *table d'hôte* and many guests. But the consciousness of new clothes sustained him, so he held up his head, turned out his toes, and took his place, trying to look as if everything was not very new and dazzling to him.

Two elderly ladies sat opposite, and he heard one

say to the other in bad Italian, "Behold the lovely boy, Maria; I should like to paint him."

And the other answered, "We will be amiable to him, and perhaps we may get him for a model. Just what I want for a little Saint John."

Tino smiled at them till his black eyes sparkled and his white teeth shone, for he understood and enjoyed their praise. The artistic ladies smiled back, and watched him with interest long after he had forgotten them, for that dinner was a serious affair to the boy, with a heavy silver spoon and fork to manage, a napkin to unfold, and three glasses to steer clear of for fear of a general upset, so awkward did he feel.

Every one else was too busy to mind his mistakes; and the ladies set them down to bashfulness, as he got red in the face, and dared not look up after spilling his soup and dropping a roll.

Presently, while waiting for dessert, he forgot himself in something Mario was saying to his neighbor on the other side: —

"A poor little fellow whom I found starving in the streets at Genoa. He has a voice; I have a heart, and I adore music. I took him to myself, and shall do my best for him. Ah, yes! in this selfish world one must not forget the helpless and the poor."

Tino stared, wondering what other boy the good signor had befriended, and was still more bewildered when Mario turned to him with a paternal air, to add in that pious tone so new to the boy, —

"This is my little friend, and he will gladly come and sing to your young ladies after dinner. Many thanks for the honor; I shall bring him out at my parlor concerts, and so fit him for his place by and by. Bow and smile, quick!"

The last words were in a sharp whisper; and Tino obeyed with a sudden bow of the head that sent his curls over his eyes, and then laughed such a boyish laugh as he shook them back that the gentleman leaning forward to look at him joined in it, and the ladies smiled sympathetically as they pushed a dish of bonbons nearer to him. Mario gave him an indulgent look, and went on in the same benevolent tone telling all he meant to do, till the kindly gentleman from Rome was much interested, having lads of his own and being fond of music.

Tino listened to the fine tales told of him and hoped no one would ask him about Genoa, for he would surely betray that he had never been there and could not lie as glibly as Mario did. He felt rather like the little old woman who did not know whether she was herself or not, but consoled himself by smiling at the ladies and eating a whole plateful of little cakes standing near him.

When they rose, Tino made his bow, and Mario walked down the long hall with his hand on the boy's shoulder and a friendly air very impressive to the spectators, who began at once to gossip about the pretty lad and his kind protector, just as the cunning gentleman planned to have them.

As soon as they were out of sight, Mario's manner changed; and telling Tino to sit down and digest his dinner or he wouldn't be able to sing a note, he went to the balcony to smoke till the servant came to conduct them to Conte Alborghetti's salon.

"Now mind, boy; do exactly as I tell you, or I'll drop you like a hot chestnut and leave you to get home as you can," said Mario, in a sharp whisper, as they paused on the threshold of the door.

"I will, signor, indeed I will!" murmured Tino, scared by the flash of his master's black eye and the grip of his hand, as he pulled the bashful boy forward.

In they went, and for a moment Tino only perceived a large light room full of people, who all looked at him as he stood beside Mario with his guitar slung over his shoulder, red cheeks, and such a flutter at his heart that he felt sure he could never sing there. The amiable host came to meet and present them to a group of ladies, while a flock of children drew near to look at and listen to the "nice singing boy from Genoa."

Mario, having paid his thanks and compliments in his best manner, opened the little concert by a grand piece upon the piano, proving that he was a fine musician, though Tino already began to fancy he was not quite so good a man as he wished to appear. Then he sang several airs from operas; and Tino forgot himself in listening delightedly to the mellow voice of his master, for the lad loved music and had never heard any like this before.

When Tino's turn came, he had lost his first shyness, and though his lips were dry and breath short, and he gave the guitar an awkward bang against the piano as he pulled it round ready to play upon, the curiosity in the faces of the children and the kindly interest of the ladies gave him courage to start bravely off with "Bella Monica," — the easiest as well as gayest of his songs. It went well; and with each verse his voice grew clearer, his hand firmer, and his eyes fuller of boyish pleasure in his own power to please.

For please he did, and when he ended with a loud twang and kissed his hand to the audience as he always used to do to the girls at home, every one clapped heartily, and the gentlemen cried, "Bravo, piccolo! He sings in truth like a little nightingale; encore, encore!"

These were sweet sounds to Tino; and he needed no urging to sing "Lucia" in his softest tones, "looking like one of Murillo's angels!" as a young lady said, while he sang away with his eyes piously lifted in the manner Mario had taught him.

Then followed a grand march from the master while the boy rested; after which Tino gave more folk-songs, and ended with a national air in which all joined like patriotic and enthusiastic Italians, shouting the musical chorus, "Viva Italia!" till the room rang.

Tino quite lost his head at that, and began to prance as if the music had got into his heels. Before Mario could stop him, he was showing one of the little girls how to dance the Salterello as the peasants dance it during Carnival; and all the children were capering gayly about the wide polished floor with Tino strumming and skipping like a young fawn from the woods.

The elder people laughed and enjoyed the pretty sight till trays of ices and bonbons came in; and the little party ended in a general enjoyment of the good things children most delight in. Tino heard his master receiving the compliments of the company, and saw the host slip a paper into his hand; but, boylike, he contented himself with a pocket full of sweetmeats, and the entreaties of his little patrons to come again soon, and so backed out of the room, after bowing till he was dizzy, and bumping against a marble table in a very painful manner.

"Well, how do you like the life I promised you? Is it all I said? Do we begin to fill our pockets, and enjoy ourselves even sooner than I expected?" asked Mario, with a good-natured slap of the shoulder, as they reached his apartment again.

"It is splendid! I like it much, very much! and I thank you with all my heart," cried Tino, gratefully kissing the hand that could tweak sharply, as well as caress when things suited its owner.

"You did well, even better than I hoped; but in some things we must improve. Those legs must be taught to keep still; and you must not forget that you are a peasant when among your betters. It passed very well to-night with those little persons, but in some places it would have put me in a fine scrape. Capers! but I feared at one moment you would have embraced the young contessa, when she danced with you."

Mario laughed as poor Tino blushed and stammered, "But, signor, she was so little, only ten years old, and I thought no harm to hold her up on that slippery floor. See, she gave me all these, and bade me come again. I would gladly have kissed her, she was so like little Annina at home."

"Well, well, no harm is done; but I see the pretty brown girls down yonder have spoiled you, and I shall have to keep an eye on my gallant young troubadour. Now to bed, and don't make yourself ill with all those confections. Felice notte, Don Giovanni!" and away went Mario to lose at play every franc of the money the generous count had given him "for the poor lad."

That was the beginning of a new and charming life for Tino, and for two months he was a busy and a happy boy, with only a homesick fit now and then when Mario was out of temper, or Luigi put more than his fair share of work upon his shoulders. The parlor concerts went well, and the little nightingale was soon a favorite toy in many salons. Night after night Tino sang and played, was petted and praised, and then trotted home to dream feverishly of new delights; for this exciting life was fast spoiling the simple lad who used to be so merry and busy at Valrose. The more he had, the more he wanted, and soon grew discontented, jealous, and peevish. He had cause to complain of some things; for none of the money earned ever came to him, and when he plucked up courage to ask for his promised share, Mario told him he only earned his food and clothes as yet. Then Tino rebelled, and got a beating, which made him outwardly as meek as a lamb, but inwardly a very resentful, unhappy boy, and spoiled all his pleasure in music and success.

He was neglected all day and left to do what he liked till needed at night, so he amused himself by lounging about the hotel or wandering on the beach to watch the fishermen cast their nets. Lazy Luigi kept him doing errands when he could; but for hours the boy saw neither master nor man, and wondered where they were. At last he found out, and his dream of fame and fortune ended in smoke.

Christmas week was a gay one for everybody, and Tino thought good times had come again; for he sang at several children's fêtes, received some pretty gifts from the kind Alborghettis, and even Mario was amiable enough to give him a golden napoleon after a run of good luck at the cards. Eager to show his people that he *was* getting on, Tino begged Antoine, the friendly waiter who had already written one letter to Stella for him, to write another, and send by a friend going that way a little parcel containing the money for Mariuccia, a fine Roman sash for Stella, and many affectionate messages to all his old friends.

It was well he had that little satisfaction, for it was his last chance to send good news or exult over his grand success. Troubles came with the new year; and in one week our poor little jay found himself stripped of all his borrowed plumes, and left a very forlorn bird indeed.

Trotting about late at night in silk stockings, and getting wet more than once in the winter rains, gave Tino a bad cold. No one cared for it; and he was soon as hoarse as a crow. His master forced him to sing several times in spite of the pain he suffered, and when at the last concert he broke down completely, Mario swore at him for "a useless brat," and began to talk of going to Milan to find a new set of singers and patrons. Had Tino been older, he would have discovered some time sooner that Signor Mario was losing favor in Nice, as he seldom paid a bill, and led a very gay, extravagant life. But, boylike, Tino saw only his own small troubles, and suspected nothing when Luigi one day packed up the velvet suit and took it away "to be repaired," he said. It *was* shabby, and Tino lying on the sofa with a headache and sharp cough, was glad no one ordered him to go with it, for the Tramontana was blowing, and he longed for old Mariuccia's herb tea and Stella's cosseting, being quite ill by this time.

That night as he lay awake in his closet coughing, feverish and restless, he heard his master and Luigi moving about till very late, evidently packing for Paris or Milan, and Tino wondered if he would like either place better than Nice, and wished they were not so far from Valrose. In the midst of his meditations he fell asleep, and when he woke, it was morning. He hurried up and went out to see what the order of the day was to be, rather pleased at the idea of travelling about the world.

To his surprise no breakfast appeared; the room was in confusion, every sign of Mario had vanished but empty bottles and a long hotel bill lying unpaid upon the table. Before Tino could collect his wits, Antoine came flying in to say with wild gesticulations and much French wrath that "the rascal Mario had gone in the night, leaving immense debts behind him, and the landlord in an apoplexy of rage."

Poor Tino was so dismayed he could only sit and let the storm pelt about his ears; for not only did the waiter appear, but the chambermaid, the coachman, and at last the indignant host himself, all scolding at once as they rummaged the rooms, questioned the bewildered boy, and wrung their hands over the escape of these dishonest wretches.

"You also, little beast, have grown fat upon my good fare! and who is to pay me for all you have eaten, not to mention the fine bed, the washing, the candles, and the coaches you have had? Ah, great heavens! what is to become of us when such things occur?" and the poor landlord tore his hair with one hand while he shook his other fist at Tino.

"Dear sir, take all I have; it is only an old guitar, and a few clothes. Not a centime do I own; but I will work for you. I can clean saucepans and run errands. Speak for me, Antoine; you are my only friend now."

The lad looked so honest and ill and pathetic, as he spoke with his poor hoarse voice, and looked beseechingly about him, that Antoine's kind heart was melted, and he advised the boy to slip away home as soon as possible, and so escape all further violence and trouble. He slipped two francs into Tino's empty pocket, and as soon as the room was cleared, helped him tie up the few old clothes that remained. The host carried off the guitar as the only thing he could seize, so Tino had less to take away than he brought, when Antoine led him out by the back way, with a good sandwich of bread and meat for his breakfast, and bade him go to the square and try to beg a ride to Valrose on some of the carriages often going thither on the way to Genoa.

With many thanks Tino left the great hotel, feeling too miserable to care much what became of him, for all his fine dreams were spoiled like the basket of china the man kicked over in the "Arabian Nights," while dreaming he was a king. How could he go home, sick, poor, and forsaken, after all the grand tales he had lately told in his letter? How they would laugh at him, the men and girls at the factory! How Mariuccia would wag her old head and say, "Ecco! is it not as I foretold?" Even Stella would weep over him and be sorry to see her dear boy in such a sad plight, yet what could he do? His voice was gone and his guitar, or he might sing about the streets, as Mario described his doing at Genoa, and so earn his daily bread till something turned up. Now he was quite helpless, and much against his will, he went to see if any chance of getting home appeared.

The day was showery, and no party was setting off for the famous drive along the Cornice road. Tino was glad of it, and went to lie on a bench at the café where he had often been with Luigi. His head ached, and his cough left him no peace, so he spent some of his money in syrup and water to quell the trouble, and with the rest paid for a good dinner and supper.

He told his sad tale to the cook, and was allowed to sleep in the kitchen after scrubbing saucepans to pay for it. But no one wanted him; and in the morning, after a cup of coffee and a roll he found himself cast upon the world again. He would not beg, and as dinner time approached, hunger reminded him of a humble friend whom he had forgotten in his own days of plenty.

He loved to stroll along the beach, and read the names on the boats drawn up there, for all were the names of saints; and it was almost as good as going to church to read the long list of Saint Brunos, Saint Francises, and Saint Ursulas. Among the fishermen was one who had always a kind word for the lad, who enjoyed a sail or a chat with Marco whenever nothing better turned up to amuse his leisure hours. Now in his trouble he remembered him, and went to the beach to ask help, for he felt ill as well as sad and hungry.

Yes, there sat the good fellow eating the bread and macaroni his little daughter had brought for his dinner, and a smile welcomed poor Tino as he sat down beside this only friend to tell his story.

Marco growled in his black beard and shook his knife with an awful frown when he heard how the lad had been deserted. Then he smiled, patted Tino's back, thrust the copper basin of food into one hand and a big lump of the brown-bread into the other, inviting him to eat in such a cordial way that the poor meal tasted better than the dainty fare at the hotel.

A draught of red wine from the gourd cheered Tino up, as did the good and kind words, and when Marco bade him go home with little Manuela to the good wife, he gladly went, feeling that he must lie down somewhere, his head was so giddy and the pain in the breast so sharp.

Buxom Teresa received him kindly, put him straight to bed in her own boy's little room, laid a cool cloth on his hot head, a warm one on his aching chest, and left him to sleep, much comforted by her motherly care. It was well the good soul befriended him, for he needed help sorely, and would have fared ill if those humble folk had not taken him in.

For a week or two he lay in Beppo's bed burning with fever, and when he could sit up again, was too feeble to do anything but smile gratefully and try to help Manuela mend nets. Marco would hear of no thanks, saying, "Good deeds bring good luck. Behold my haul of fish each day thou hast been here, poverino! I am well paid, and Saint Peter will bless my boat for thy sake."

Tino was very happy in the little dark, shabby house that smelt of onions, fish, and tar, was full of brown children, and the constant clack of Teresa's lively tongue as she gossiped with her neighbors, or fried polenta for the hungry mouths that never seemed filled.

But the time came when Tino could go about and then begged for work, anxious to be independent and earn a little so that in the spring he could go home without empty pockets.

"I have taken thought for thee, my son, and work warm and easy is ready if thou wilt do it. My friend, Tommaso Neri, makes the good macaroni near by. He needs a boy to mind the fire and see to the donkey who grinds below there. Food, shelter, and such wages as thou art able to earn, he will give thee. Shall it be?"

Tino gratefully accepted, and with hearty embraces all round went off one day to see his new place. It was in the old part of Nice, a narrow, dirty street, a little shop with one window full of the cheaper sorts of this favorite food of all Italians, and behind the shop a room where an old woman sat spinning while two little boys played with pine cones and pretty bits of marble at her feet.

A fat jolly man, with a shining face and loud voice, greeted Marco and the lad, saying he "was worn to a thread with much work, since that bad imp of a donkey-boy had run away leaving the blessed macaroni to spoil, and poor Carmelita to perish for want of care. Come below at once, and behold the desolation of the place."

With that he led the way to the cellar, where a small furnace-fire burned, and an old gray donkey went round and round, turning a wheel which set some unseen machinery in motion with a dismal creaking sound. Down through many holes in one part of the wooden floor overhead came long pipes of macaroni, hardening as they hung quivering in the hot air till stiff enough to be cut off in handfuls and laid to dry on wire trays over the furnace.

Tino had never seen the good macaroni made before, and was much interested in the process, though it was of the rudest kind. In a room upstairs a great vat of flour and water was kept stirring round and round and forced down to the place below by the creaking wheel which patient Carmelita turned all day. The cellar was dark but warm; and Tino felt that it would be comfortable there with the old donkey for a comrade, jolly Tommaso for a master, and enough to eat, — for it was evident the family lived well, so plump and shining were all the faces, so cheery the tempers of the old women and little lads.

There Marco left him, well satisfied that he had done his best for the poor boy; and there Tino lived for three months, busy, well fed, and contented, till spring sunshine made him long for the sweet air, the green fields, and dear faces at Valrose. Tommaso was lazy but kind, and if the day's work was done in time, let Tino out to see Marco's children or to run on the beach with little Jacopo and Seppi. The grandmother gave him plenty of rye bread, thin wine, and macaroni fried in oil; old Carmelita learned to love him and to lean her gray head on his shoulder with joyful waggings of her long ears as he caressed her, and each week increased the little hoard in an old shoe hidden behind a beam.

But it was a dull life for a boy who loved music, flowers, light, and freedom; and he soon grew tired of seeing only a procession of legs go by the low windows level with the street; the creak of the wheel was not half so welcome as the brisk rattle of the mill at home, and the fat little lads always climbing over him could not be so dear as sister Stella and pretty Annina, the wine-maker's daughter, at Valrose. Even the kind old woman who often saved an orange for him, and gave him a gay red cotton handkerchief on his birthday, was less to his taste than Mariuccia, who adored him in spite of her scolding and stern ways.

So he looked about for travellers going to Genoa; and one happy day as he returned from church, he saw, sitting under two red umbrellas before two easels beside the road, the two elderly ladies of the hotel. Both wore brown hats like mushrooms; both had gray curls bobbing in the wind; and both were painting away for dear life, trying to get a good sketch of the ruined gateway, where passion-flowers climbed, and roses nodded through the bars.

Tino stopped to look, as many another passerby had done; and glancing up to see if he admired their work, the good ladies recognized their "Saint John," as they called the pretty boy who had vanished before they could finish the pictures they had begun of him.

They were so glad to see him that he opened his heart to them, and found to his great joy that in a week they were to drive to Genoa, and would gladly take him along if he would sit to them meantime. Of course he agreed, and ran home to tell his master that he must go. Tommaso bewailed his loss, but would not keep him; and as Marco's son Beppo was willing to take his place till another lad could be found, Tino was free to sit in a sheepskin for the Misses Blair as often as they liked.

It was a very happy week; and when the long-desired day came at last, Tino was so gay he danced and sang till the dingy cellar seemed to be full of birds in high spirits. Poor Carmelita gratefully ate the cabbage he gave her as a farewell offering; the old woman found her box full of favorite snuff; and each small boy grew more shiny than ever over a new toy presented by Tino. Tommaso wept as he held him in his fat arms, and gave him a bundle of half-baked macaroni as a reward for his faithful service, while Marco and all his family stood at the hotel door to see the carriage depart.

"Really quite like a wedding, with all those orange-flowers and roses," said Miss Priscilla, as Teresa and Manuela threw great bunches of flowers into their laps, and kissed their hands to the departing travellers.

Sitting proudly aloft, Tino waved his old hat to these good friends till he could see them no more;

then having, with some difficulty, bestowed his long bundle from Tommaso, his basket of fish from Marco, his small parcel of clothes, and the immense bouquet the children had made for him, he gave himself up to the rapture of that lovely April day.

The kind ladies had given him a new suit of clothes like the old ones, and paid him well besides; so he felt quite content with the picturesque peasant garments he wore, having had enough of fine feathers, and gayly jingled the money in his pocket, though it was not the fortune he had foolishly hoped to make so easily. He was a wiser boy than the one who went over that road six months before, and decided that even if his voice did come back in time, he would be in no hurry to leave home till he was sure it was the wisest thing to do. He had some very serious thoughts and sensible plans in his young head, and for a time was silent and sober. But soon the delicious air, the lovely scenery, and the many questions of the ladies raised his spirits, and he chattered away till they stopped for dinner.

All that long bright day they drove along the wonderful road, and as night fell, saw Valrose lying green and peaceful in the valley as they paused on the hill-top to enjoy its beauty. Then they went slowly down to the Falcone, and the moment the luggage was taken in, rooms secured, and dinner ordered, Tino, who had been quivering with impatience, said eagerly, —

"Dear signoras, now I go to my own people to embrace them; but in the morning we come to thank you for your great kindness to me."

Miss Priscilla opened her mouth to send some message; but Tino was off like an arrow, and never stopped till he burst into the little kitchen where Mariuccia sat shelling dry beans, and Stella was packing mandarinas in dainty baskets for market. Like an affectionate little bear did the boy fall upon and embrace the two astonished women; while Stella laughed and cried, and Mariuccia called on all the saints to behold how tall and fat and beautiful her angel had become, and to thank them for restoring him to their arms. The neighbors rushed in; and till late that night there was the sound of many voices in the stone cottage under the old fig-tree.

Tino's adventures were listened to with the deepest interest, and a very hearty welcome given him. All were impressed with the splendors he had seen, afflicted by his trials, and grateful for his return. No one laughed or reproached, but regarded him as a very remarkable fellow, and predicted that whether his voice came back or not, he was born for good luck and would prosper. So at last he got to bed in the old loft, and fell asleep with the same friendly moon looking in at him as it did before, only now it saw a quiet face, a very happy heart, and a contented boy, glad to be safe again under the humble roof that was his home.

Early next morning a little procession of three went to the Falcone bearing grateful offerings to the dear signoras who sat on the portico enjoying the balmy air that blew up from the acres of flowers below. First came Tino, bearing a great basket of the delicious little oranges which one never tastes in their perfection unless one eats them fresh from the tree; then Stella with two pretty boxes of perfume; and bringing up the rear, old Mariuccia with a blue jar of her best honey, which like all that of Valrose was famous.

The ladies were much delighted with these gifts, and promised to stop and see the givers of them on their return from Genoa, if they came that way. Tino took a grateful farewell of the good souls; Stella kissed their hands, with her dark eyes full of tender thanks, and Mariuccia begged the saints to have them in their special keeping by land and by sea, for their kindness to her boy.

An hour later, as the travellers drove down the steep road from the village, they were startled by a sudden shower of violets and roses which rained upon them from a high bank beside the path. Looking up, they saw Tino and his sister laughing, waving their hands, and tossing flowers as they called in their musical language, —

"A rivederla, signoras! Grazia, grazia!" till the carriage rolled round the corner looking as if it were Carnival-time, so full was it of fragrant violets and lovely roses.

"Nice creatures! how prettily they do things! I hope we *shall* see them again; and I wonder if the boy will ever be famous. Such a pity to lose that sweet voice of his!" said Miss Maria, the younger of the sisters, as they drove along in a nest of sweet and pretty gifts.

"I hope not, for he will be much safer and happier in this charming place than wandering about the world and getting into trouble as these singers always do. *I* hope he will be wise enough to be contented with the place in which his lot is cast," answered Miss Priscilla, who knew the world and had a good old-fashioned love for home and all it gives us.

She was right; Tino *was* wise, and though his

voice did come back in time, it was no longer wonderful; and he was contented to live on at Valrose, a busy, happy, humble gardener all his life, saying with a laugh when asked about his runaway adventures, —

"Ah, I have had enough of music and macaroni; I prefer my flowers and my freedom."

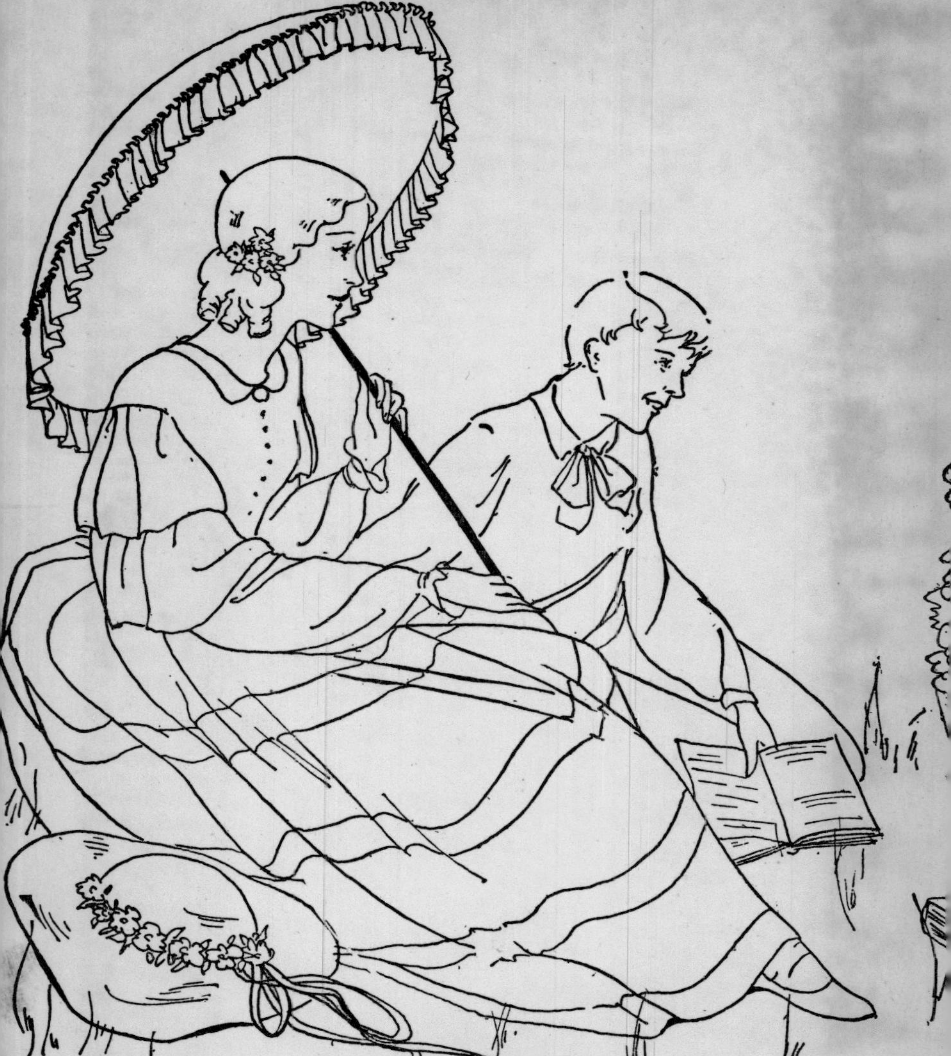